ENGINEERING
THE
AUSTRALIAN
DREAM

JAIDEEP
MANOHAR PADALWAR

First published in Australia by Aurora House

This edition published 2025
Copyright © Jaideep Manohar Padalwar 2025

Typesetting and e-book design: Amit Dey (amitdey2528@gmail.com)
Cover design: Donika Mishineva (www.artofdonika.com)

The right of Jaideep Manohar Padalwar to be identified as Author of the Work
has been asserted in accordance with the Copyright, Designs and Patents Act
1988.

ISBN number: 978-1-923298-30-9 (paperback)

A catalogue record for this
book is available from the
NATIONAL
LIBRARY   National Library of Australia
OF AUSTRALIA

DEDICATION

To my parents, Manohar Padalwar and Chhaya Padalwar, for instilling confidence in me by encouraging me to face challenging situations, also for their support and belief in my dreams.

To my brother, Amar, for being my pillar of strength, always encouraging me—without saying a word—to rise above difficulties.

To my wife, Rutuja, whose faith in my ability inspired me to write and share my story.

To my daughter, Arya, as she is the reason why I wrote this book.

To my friends, Ashutosh, Mihir, Vishnu, Jayesh, Tushar, Vikram, Mazhar, Vishal, Govind, Rigved, Rohit, Suyash, Ajeet, Ryan, Sava etc. who helped me to overcome difficulties and supported me. Their assistance made this journey memorable.

And if you are someone who dares to dream, may this story remind you that every step, no matter how small, brings you closer to your aspirations.

CONTENTS

PROLOGUE

"So, you're leaving in seven days." Vishnu, my dear friend, asks. We rarely meet these days—he's been in Glasgow for the past three years. But distance never weakens true friendship.

"Yes, I am."

"Where did you get the guts for this?" he laughs, shaking his head.

"I don't know ... but honestly, I'm scared as hell."

"Don't be scared now. The time for fear has passed. Now is the time to do." he says.

"True."

"What will you miss the most?"

"My brother." I say without hesitation. "I should be here with him, but I'm leaving. My parents, my friends ... and this stupid pink building where we have countless memories. Far enough and close to heart." I pause, looking up at the structure that has been the backdrop to so many of my dreams. "This is where my dream took shape."

We let the silence settle in, absorbing the weight of my words.

Then I ask, "You just came back from Glasgow. Why?"

"I'm the only child. I had to come back."

"Then you can understand." I say. "Having a younger sibling gives you extra confidence. My brother is a genius—I'm leaving my parents in better hands."

Vishnu nods, understanding the unspoken emotions behind my words. Then he asks, "But why Australia?"

"Cricket. The scenery. I don't know … I just feel like I need to be there."

"You have a good life in India, too."

"I know. But it's too comfortable now. I know I'm good at my work, people rate me highly … but I need something more. I want the challenge of proving myself in a completely different world. I can't even speak English fluently—that's another challenge. And that excites me."

"But it'll be tough at first. Expect the worst."

"I know." I say, taking a deep breath. "But I'm ready to explore my uncomfortable zone."

NAÏVE DESIRES

"My heart wants what it wants." I said, my gaze flickering between the cricket match on TV and my mum. I sat beside Dad, watching an India vs. Australia game in Sydney from our warm, happy home in suburban Mumbai.

"And what's your new desire now?" Dad asked.

"I want to go to Australia and live there." I said, voicing a decision I'd already made in my heart.

"Hmm." Dad murmured.

"Don't say that! I'll prove it to you." I shot back.

"You just say things. Your desires change every day." Dad said with a slight smile.

"No, they don't. My desires—they just build up, one after another, never really changing, just adding to the list."

"I'm tired of listening to your dreams." Mum sighed. "Just be happy wherever you are, and always stay close to people who love you."

I leaned forward, my voice firm. "I'll be happy when I fulfil all my desires. I have only a few, which I will achieve in stages."

"Remember the time you wanted to be a cricketer and play for India?" Dad said.

"Yes, I do. That dream has never left me. There's something about the way this sport brings out raw emotions in people. I want to be at the heart of that, to be the one spreading joy and unity through my actions on the field. I imagine newsagencies flooded with people eager to read about me. And when they do, it would make readers walk with their heads held high. I dream of being interviewed by famous hosts at award shows."

"Is that all you want?" Mum asked.

"No, that's not all. I don't just want to play for India; I want to be the captain of the Indian cricket team. Under my leadership, we would win test series in Australia, England, South Africa, New Zealand, Pakistan and the West Indies. We'd lift the World Cup multiple times and make India proud. And I want to be a role model. I'd love to see kids imitating my actions, talking about me before every game. I want to be the reason for families to bond, to see Hindus and Muslims hug and forget their differences."

"Is that why you wanted to be a cricketer? It sounds like you're chasing the spotlight." Dad said.

"No, all those things are just by-products. I'd love the constant hustle and adapting to challenges every day. And the complexities—the science, numbers, strategies, reactions, mind-games, dedication, preparation, focus, even the sledging—it all excites me."

"But last week, you wanted to become an electrical engineer." Mum said. "Do you want to be an engineer or a cricketer?"

"Dad has a diploma in electrical engineering. I just want to prove I'm better than him." I said, pointing at him. "That's why I want a bachelor's in electrical engineering. One step above Dad."

"Why do you want to be better than me?" Dad asked.

"You always told me to aim for the highest. After every exam result, when I showed you my report card, you'd ask how many classmates scored higher than me. If I told you how many scored less, you'd start ranting because I wasn't aiming high enough."

"What about a PhD, then? You said you want to do that, too." Dad continued. "But I won't pay for it."

"Mum wants me to be a doctor. She gets upset when I say I want to be an engineer."

"So, is a PhD a substitute for becoming a doctor?"

"It's the same title, but it means something different. Both of us will be happy." I said.

Dad laughed at my naïvety. "And what about a master's?"

"What about it?"

"You said you want to do a master's. Why?"

"When I went back to school after the summer break, we were greeted by the new principal. He spoke with such authority. On the first day back, I saw workers placing a big block of black marble on the wall in front of the principal's office. We were puzzled. The next day, we saw the principal's name and qualifications carved on it in golden letters. The list was long—nine qualifications, including a bachelor's, a master's, a PhD, a post-doctorate and some others. That's why I want a master's."

"And what about Australia? Why do you want to go there?" Mum asked.

"Mum! Don't interrupt when two people are conversing."

Mum and Dad burst out laughing, though I wasn't sure why. "Okay, sorry. But really, why do you want to go to Australia?"

"Dad works at British Oxygen Company (BOC), right? I saw a BOC truck in Sydney just now on TV, driving smoothly along a road perfectly situated between the blue ocean and light green grassland. To be better than Dad, I'll work at BOC in Australia. So, I've decided I must settle in Australia. Also, Australia always wins in cricket, so the whole country must be full of winners. If I'm with winners, I'll become a leader one day, too."

"If you want to settle overseas, try America, Dubai or Europe. We know people living in those countries." Dad said.

"No, I said I'll go to Australia."

"Well, you'll have to grow up and pay for it yourself." Dad said.

The match resumed after a break, and we turned our attention back to the game. India lost the match, and like the rest of the country, Dad and I were very disappointed.

At the end of the day, Dad said, "Becoming a cricketer isn't easy. You have to work hard, and even then, you could face losses like this."

"Okay then. I'll drop my plan to become a cricketer and just focus on going to Australia."

"Australia is uncharted territory for us. You'd be on your own, with no support, no familiar faces to guide you. It'd be a much tougher path than you realise. To settle anywhere, you must start from the bottom. Only then can you understand the culture and basic functioning. It's scary to go somewhere where you don't know anyone."

"*Dar ke aage jeet hai.*" I said. "Beyond fear lies victory."

SUPPORT, BELIEF AND CONFIDENCE

"Can I play cricket now? We can go where you want after I finish in an hour." I asked, looking longingly at the playground filled with familiar faces. I squeezed my mum's hand, hoping for a positive response.

"Playtime is from 6 p.m. to 7 p.m. only." Mum replied.

"But all my friends are playing now." I said.

"These aren't your friends." she said, her tone final.

"I know him, him and him." I pointed to a few of my friends, not giving up.

"All right, but not now. We have something important to do." she said, continuing our walk.

"Okay, but you'll let me play from 6 to 7?"

"Yes."

We walked past a small temple. I couldn't help but smile as a memory surfaced. Mum caught my expression and asked, "Why are you smiling? What's going on in your head?"

"It's nothing." I shrugged.

"Share your happiness!" she said.

"Every time I walk by this building, I remember when someone hit a ball that bounced off the road and hit the temple bell.

There were almost 50 kids playing, and we all cheered. That memory makes me smile."

"Nice!" she gave a warm smile.

After a few more blocks, we reached another playground with slides and swings.

"Mummy, can I go down the slide once?" I asked.

"Okay, just once." she agreed, as it didn't require a detour.

I climbed up the ladder and slid down quickly, with Mum waiting for me. I then asked, "Can I play on the swing for a while?"

"We'll do it on the way back." she said, gently guiding me along.

"Okay." Then I spotted a balloon vendor. "Mummy, I want a balloon."

"We'll get it on the way back."

"Where are we going?" I asked, curiosity taking over.

"To the temple. To meet God." she said.

"Which temple are we going to?"

"Shiva's temple."

"What language does Shiva understand?"

"God understands every language." she said.

"Seriously? That can't be right. How can someone know all languages? I only know Hindi, and I'm learning English in school, but I can't speak it yet."

"He can understand everything. That's why everyone prays to Him. He can also listen to your feelings and help you get anything and everything."

"Understand everyone's feelings? And grant every wish? That doesn't sound very promising." I said.

"Try it and see for yourself."

"Things I want aren't easy. I'll have to wait a long time." I said.

"Ask for something simple, just to test your belief." she said.

"Hmm, let me think of something easy."

We walked past a petrol station where people were honking in frustration.

"Mum, why are people honking so loudly?" I asked while sticking my fingers in my ears.

"The world is filled with chaos. That is why people follow religion, to find peace." Mum replied.

Escaping the chaos, we finally reached the temple. Imitating others, I removed my shoes, washed my feet and touched the temple stairs as a sign of respect. I jumped, trying to reach the overhanging bell, while Mum chatted with another devotee.

"Mummy, I want to ring the bell. Pick me up." I tugged at her hand.

She lifted me, and I pushed the bell's handle as hard as I could. The loud, resonating sound filled the temple, filling me with pure joy. Smiling, Mum set me down, and we walked towards the idol.

I approached the sanctum, closed my eyes, joined my hands and whispered, "I want a candy." It seemed like a simple test for the deity.

I opened my eyes, noticing Mum still deep in prayer. Her list was longer than mine. After a few moments, she finished and pointed towards the priest offering small portions of food to all devotees as a blessing. I took some and looked at Mum, waiting for what was next. She started walking towards the exit, and I followed, already thinking about the things I'd do on the way back.

Just a few feet from the door, she stopped, turned, and asked me to sit next to her, facing the idol. "Close your eyes, think about God, and keep repeating your wishes." she said.

"Why? I'll wait to see if my first wish comes true." I said.

"Okay, but for mental peace, just sit here and think of God." she said.

I closed my eyes, hearing the sounds of people moving and the bell ringing in the background.

After a while, Mum said, "Open your eyes." bringing me out of my meditative state.

"Are we leaving now?"

"Yes, we are."

As we walked towards the door, Mum said, "Walk backwards towards the exit."

"I've seen people do that. Why?"

"We should knowingly never show our back to God."

"What happens if we do?"

"God might be upset with us."

"There are so many people. How do you know He's looking at me?"

"God is omnipresent. He sees everything and everyone." Mum said. I nodded.

On our way back, Mum surprised me by saying, "Get something for yourself from the shop."

This had never happened before. Was it God or just a coincidence? Maybe He was listening to me. I didn't ask too many questions and bought a candy, enjoying every bite.

Since then, I began making a series of wishes. Every Saturday, we'd walk to the temple, I'd make a wish and wait for it to come true. It became a habit to think of new wishes every week, so I often asked for focus on my studies or better marks in exams. Occasionally, I wished for tangible things.

Once, I asked God to help India win a Cricket World Cup in my lifetime. I'm not sure if it was just my wish or a billion others, but it came true a decade later.

Another time, I asked for my own Monopoly board game, and weeks later, I received it as a gift.

I then wished for a cricket bat and soon forgot about it. Months later, I sat for a scholarship test that could secure government funding for my education. The exam was in two phases, with a break in between. During the break, Dad and I went to a nearby shopping centre, where we stumbled upon a cricket shop. My dad, who also loved cricket, couldn't resist stepping inside.

As I browsed, I found a bat that felt just right—a Kookaburra with a green sticker, perfect grip, and a solid bulge in the middle. I practised a few imaginary shots with it, feeling the balance.

"You like it?" Dad asked.

"Yes, very much!" I expected him to tell me to score well in the exam before getting it.

But to my surprise, he said, "Come to the counter." and bought the bat. I wanted to ask why, but I didn't want to spoil the moment. I realised then that God works in mysterious ways.

I love my parents deeply, though I find it hard to express my feelings. They've always provided for me, supported me and equipped me with the tools to succeed in life.

As I grew older, the thought of going to Australia lingered in my mind. I wondered if I could enjoy being so far away from them. Could I leave them alone when they might need help? Financial support wouldn't be enough. I needed God to provide a solution. I asked God for a brother who can take their responsibility when I was away.

When I was nine, my uncle (Mum's brother), aunt and cousin came to visit and we spent a happy time together. I had no idea what was about to unfold.

One Monday morning, as I got ready for school, Dad said, "You're not going to school today."

"Why?"

"We have to take Mum to the hospital."

"What happened?"

"She isn't feeling well." he said.

I was worried and couldn't understand what was going on. I just wanted her to get better so we could play together again.

"What happened to Mum?" I asked my aunt.

"The doctor will let us know." She smiled to reassure me.

At the hospital, my parents left me with my uncle and aunt. I asked them, "Will she be all right?"

They nodded casually. "Yes."

Soon after, a nurse came out, followed by my dad, who told me, "You've got a brother to play with now."

I was ecstatic! I'd wished for a brother and it had come true. I ran around shouting, "I've got a brother! I've got a brother!" to everyone who'd listen. I felt I was the happiest person on the planet.

A few months later at school, we were given an essay to write on the topic of the happiest moment of our lives.

One friend said, "I'll write about my last birthday."

Another countered, "I'll write about the place I visited last summer."

Someone else added, "I'll write about the time I got a bicycle."

When it was my turn, I said, "I'll write about when brother was born."

"Whose brother?" a friend asked.

"My neighbour's!" I replied sarcastically, then added sincerely, "Obviously, mine."

"What's his name?" asked a friend.

"Amar." I replied.

The next week, our English teacher asked us to show our homework. As she checked everyone's work, she reached my desk and asked, "Where's your homework?"

"I forgot and left my notebook at home." I lied confidently.

"Have you done it?"

"Yes."

"Good, bring it tomorrow." she said.

That day at our 15-minute recess, I sat alone, planning how to finish this essay in such a short time. My friend noticed and asked, "What happened?"

"I'll finish my essay now. We were given a week, and I kept postponing it." I admitted.

"Oh, no problem. It's good you planned the topic. Want to play after?" my friend asked.

"Sure." I said, hoping to join them soon. But I got so engrossed in my writing that I missed recess entirely. I wrote about when Amar was born and handed it to the teacher the next day.

"That's a beautiful essay, Jaideep. Keep it up!" she praised, making me proud.

———⬦⬦⬦———

Some years later, Amar, Dad and I were watching television one evening when Mum walked in. "There's a man in town named Kalia. He's a skilled fortune-teller." she said.

"I'm not going." I said.

"I don't need to go." added Amar.

"I'll never visit that man." Dad said, firmly crossing his arms.

Mum, unfazed, persisted, "You all have wishes you're working hard to achieve. Someday, you'll need a bit of luck."

"Luck doesn't even come close to me." Dad said with a sarcastic smile.

"Luck hates me. It's simple; I'm not going." I said.

"I don't need any more good luck." Amar said.

A few days passed, and unexpectedly, Dad announced, "I'm visiting Kalia tomorrow."

Amar and I couldn't help but laugh. Dad, who had been so adamantly against the idea, had succumbed to the idea. He'd even mocked Mum for suggesting it. Yet, here he was, preparing to go.

The following day, Dad visited Kalia and diligently followed the tasks he'd been assigned. He began by waking up earlier than usual to worship God and chant sacred names. As part of the ritual, he poured some oil onto a plant in front of our apartment building. To our surprise, a month later, the issue he'd been struggling with was unexpectedly resolved. He received a promotion at work, enabling him to buy an apartment for us. His wishes had come true, instilling a newfound sense of belief in all of us.

One fine day, Mum approached me with the same proposition, "Let's visit Kalia." After Dad's experience, I couldn't resist trying it myself.

"Okay." I agreed.

We walked to his place, which was in a townhouse complex. His was the first house on the right as we entered the complex, with a giant brown steel door that immediately caught my attention.

"He must be wealthy." I thought. After the first door, there was another one. "Oh, he's very wealthy."

In my mind, I pictured his house with red interiors and heavy red curtains, like the ones I'd seen in movies. I expected a stereotypical fortune-teller—bald, short, with a round face, a tilak on his forehead and dressed in orange robes.

When I knocked, Kalia himself opened the door. His appearance was a complete surprise. He was a big man with light grey hair, fair skin and broad shoulders who towered over me. He wore glasses, a light blue shirt, and white pants—completely different from the image I had conjured up.

"Welcome." Kalia greeted us.

"Namaste." my mum replied, while I simply gave him a look of teenage arrogance mixed with scepticism and a fake smile.

He nodded, acknowledging my attitude without a word. His office, painted a soothing light green, featured a statue of Ganesh prominently displayed on the desk, surrounded by numerous books, a computer, a printer and chairs.

"This is my eldest son." Mum said, pointing at me as if there were other people in the room.

"What is your name?" Kalia asked.

"Jaideep."

"What school do you attend?"

"DAV Public School."

"Good. Which standard?"

"7th Standard."

"Which subjects do you like?"

"Maths and science."

"What about English, Hindi, Marathi?"

"Nah, I don't like those." I shook my head.

"Why not?"

"They're too subjective. In those subjects, quantity matters more than quality. I have to write too many words for each answer to score good marks."

"And why do you like Maths and Science?"

"Maths and science are objective, unlike languages. Quality is more important than quantity. It's much easier to prove things that make sense."

"What about history and civics?"

"History requires too much memorisation, and civics is all about politics. I have no interest in politics."

"History teaches us important lessons. We can learn from the good deeds of great leaders and avoid their mistakes." Kalia explained calmly.

"But the history we're learning is too old. We'll never have the chance to replicate those deeds or mistakes." I said.

"If we know our history, we can be better at predicting the future." Kalia said.

"That's why we're here today. Mum said you can see the future and help me avoid any problems I might encounter." I said casually, to test his credibility.

Kalia merely responded with a calm smile, "Knowledge is always useful. It never goes to waste. Everything you learn can be applied in various ways."

"I'm more concerned about marks." I said.

"What do you want to become when you leave school?".

"An engineer."

"Why engineering?" Kalia's voice held genuine curiosity.

"Because my dad has a diploma in electrical engineering. I have to do better than him." I said.

Kalia smiled at my arrogance and glanced at my mum. "How can I help?" he asked her.

"He has anger issues." Mum said. "He gets very angry at home, but he's sweet outside."

"Anger is common among teenagers nowadays." Kalia said, reassuring her that it wasn't a serious issue.

"But it causes unrest at home." Mum continued. "When he's happy, everyone is happy. But when he gets upset, it spoils the mood for everyone."

"No problem." Kalia said. "What is his date and time of birth?" His right hand hovered over the keyboard, ready to enter the details.

Mum told him and Kalia entered it into his system. As we waited for my birth chart to compile, my heart started pounding. I was nervous about what my future might hold. I wasn't great at studies, useless at sports and had no other career prospects in mind. My future seemed bleak, and I wondered whether I had the skills or resources to achieve my ambitions. My mind raced with anxiety so I silently chanted God's name, "Ram, Ram, Ram." hoping for reassurance.

After a few minutes, Kalia spoke. "Everything in his life is good. There are some issues, but there are easy solutions."

"That's good to hear." Mum said, relieved. "What are the problems?"

"The usual—fidgetiness, anxiety, nervousness, fear and anger." Kalia replied.

"What are the solutions?" Mum asked.

"Every morning, he should chant these short mantras 108 times." Kalia instructed, writing something on a piece of paper.

"What could that possibly do?" I asked.

"It's a form of meditation. It will keep your mind relaxed for the day. And chanting God's name will bring good luck and positive energy." Kalia explained as he handed the paper to Mum. "Take this to the shop, and they'll provide you with what you need."

He examined my birth chart for a few more minutes while I watched him closely, trying to read his expression. "He will study engineering." Kalia finally said.

A wave of relief washed over me. My first goal was achievable, though I felt a bit sceptical. I had told him my ambition earlier, so his prediction seemed less impressive. My heart yearned for him to say something I hadn't revealed, something that would prove his abilities.

Then Kalia added, "He will go overseas."

"Yes, he always talks about going to Australia." Mum chimed in.

Kalia nodded and continued, "It looks like he will definitely go to Australia eventually."

"But how will we manage the finances? It's so expensive to go overseas." Mum's concern was evident in her voice.

"That will be taken care of when the time comes." Kalia reassured her. "When the time is right, everything will fall into place."

I'd heard exactly what I wanted to hear. After that, nothing else mattered. Their lips moved, they glanced at me occasionally, but my mind was elsewhere. My heart was at peace, my brain relaxed. My goal was clear, and I believed my stars were aligned to guide me to my destination. Now, all I had to do was work towards it.

Amar had always supported my dream—one that would take me far from my loved ones—and Mum had given me belief. I felt a renewed enthusiasm about my ambition. Never did I think of going to any other country. But despite my newfound determination, I was still nervous about the journey ahead.

———◦◦◇◦◦———

When I was 14, one day, Dad announced, "You're going to Nanded by yourself this summer." Until then, Dad had always arranged everything and accompanied me on all my journeys. The idea of travelling alone was completely foreign to me.

"I can't do it by myself! I want someone to accompany me." I said.

"No, you have to do it yourself." Dad said.

"I don't know how to travel."

"Go to the bus stop and book a ticket yourself."

"How do I get to the bus stop?"

"Take an auto." Dad said, referring to the three-seater taxis that often squeezed in more passengers than they should.

"Who will call the auto?"

"You will."

"How do I know if the bus driver will take me to the correct place?"

"You won't know until you get there." Dad said.

"How will you know when I arrive?"

"Call us from the local phone booth."

"Okaaay ... " I said and went to book the bus tickets.

The time leading up to the journey flew by, filled with nervous anticipation.

The day of the trip arrived faster than I expected. I'd barely slept the night before. I asked Dad, "Why are you sending me alone?"

"It's your test." he said.

"What test?"

"A test of your travel sense."

"Who will give me marks for this test?"

"There are no marks. It's either pass or fail."

"What's the pass criteria?"

"You reach Nanded and return home safely."

I'd only ever travelled with my family, but going to Nanded would be my first solo trip. And as much as I feared failure, I knew I had to succeed. After all, this journey was only the beginning of a much longer road to achieving my goals.

I'd never thought much about travelling until then. After Kalia's assurance and passing Dad's test, I felt more confident I could travel independently. But I was still nervous, unsure about managing on my own.

Over the years, I have found joy in being surrounded by friends and family, all while keeping my goals alive in my mind and getting through my daily routine.

Every moment with Amar was a blessing. I would often ask him to do things I was forbidden to do, especially when it came to cricket. My family wanted me to prioritise my studies, but I couldn't resist the allure of the game. If there was a match on, I couldn't focus on anything else. My attention was always on what was happening on the field.

Our apartment was in a three-storey building, and my bedroom faced a two-lane street. Across the street stood another building, with shops on the ground floor that played music on the radio during the quiet afternoon hours. I could hear the melodies clearly every day, though the words of the songs remained a mystery.

One day, a thrilling cricket match between India and Sri Lanka was set to unfold. Both teams had won two games each, and everyone at school was buzzing with excitement. As soon as the final bell rang, no one lingered to chat—we all rushed home to catch the game. I did the same.

I climbed the three flights of stairs and rang the doorbell. Mum opened the door, surprised to see me. "How come you're home so early today?" she asked.

"Everyone left early, so no hanging out after school." I said.

"Why? What's so special today?"

"Today's the final match of the India-Sri Lanka series."

"So what?"

"It's an important game."

"There's an important game every month." she said.

"But this one is different. Both teams are strong, and it's going to be exciting."

"Last month, you said the same thing about South Africa. What's different today?"

"South Africa is better than India, but India still won. That made it special."

"And today?"

"India and Sri Lanka are equally matched. It's going to be a nail-biter."

"Okay." Mum said.

"And I really want to watch it. It's already started."

"No." she said.

"What? Why not?"

"Because it's study time. They earn millions playing the game. You get nothing except wasted time. Only if you study will you get somewhere."

"But I want to watch the game ..."

She knew exactly how to shut me up. "I'll call your dad and complain about you."

Without a word, I turned and walked to my room, my disappointment evident. Amar had overheard our conversation and was laughing at my predicament. I changed into my home clothes, wondering how to keep up with the game. I silently asked God for help.

"Go to the shop and get some milk before you start studying." Mum called out.

Normally, I would have refused out of sheer frustration, but this time, I found myself asking, "How much?"

Mum, surprised, replied, "One litre."

Annoyed at my lack of rebellion, I headed to the store nearby. "Hello, one litre of milk, please." I said to the shopkeeper, who was engrossed in the game on the radio. He didn't reply, just nodded and began measuring out the milk, all while staying absorbed in the match. He handed me the milk and said, "Ten rupees."

"I know." I muttered, handing him the money. As I started to walk away, an idea struck me. I turned back and asked, "Can you increase the volume, please?"

The shopkeeper, thinking I was annoyed, apologised, "Oh, sorry, is it bothering you?"

"No, I want you to turn it up."

He looked puzzled. "Why?"

"Because my parents won't let me watch the game. But I can hear the radio from my balcony."

Understanding dawned on him. He turned up the volume and asked, "Is this good?"

"A little more."

"Now?"

"Perfect."

I returned home with the milk, a smile playing on my lips. Mum noticed and asked, "Why are you so happy?"

"Nothing." I said, heading to my room. I locked the door, opened the window, and listened to the game through the radio from the shop. For the first three hours, I enjoyed the match in peace. Then, suddenly, the sound stopped. I rushed to the balcony and saw the shop was closed—it was past 7 p.m. I needed a new plan.

Just then, Dad came home. I overheard him asking, "He's not watching the match today, right?"

"No." Mum said. "I made sure he's studying."

I knew Dad would watch the game, so I called Amar to my room. "If you do something for me, and I'll give you a chocolate tomorrow."

Amar, then just six years old but smart enough to understand bribery, asked, "What do you want me to do?"

I handed him a small notepad and pencil. "After every over, write the score on one of these pages, tear it off, and slide it under my door."

"That's it?" he asked.

"Yes. Just make sure Mum and Dad don't find out."

Amar grinned at the thought of the chocolate and agreed. I waited by the door, listening intently for any cheers or loud commentary. Soon, I heard footsteps and saw a piece of paper slide under the door: "0/0, 1 Over."

"Nice." I whispered, relieved. This routine of listening to the radio during the day and receiving chits of scores in the evening continued for a few months. But eventually, Mum caught Amar in the act and followed him to my room. She burst in, finding me with the scores.

"What's this?" she demanded.

"Amar wanted to distract me from my studies." I said, throwing him under the bus without hesitation.

Amar, wide-eyed and shocked, protested, "No, he told me to do it!"

But Mum believed me, and Amar was dragged off by his ear. My evening scores stopped after that. But I bought his love back by offering two candies.

———◦◦◦◦◦◦———

A few years later, in 2007, Amar entered my room, his eyes filled with sadness. He hugged me tightly and said, "Don't go to Australia. It's not a safe place."

I'd seen saw the news that had upset him. "Okay." I said to calm him down. I tried to distract myself with studying.

The next morning, I found Mum in the kitchen. She looked at me and said, "Amar told you not to go to Australia, right?"

"Yes." I replied. "Do you know why?"

She sighed. "We heard on the news about racist attacks in Melbourne. A few Indians were killed. Hundreds have been attacked in Australia over the past two years. Is there any other country you're interested in?" she asked.

"If not Australia, I'll stay in India." I said.

LUCKY, BUT NOT BY ACCIDENT

Some believe destiny is set in stone, while others argue it's in our hands to shape. I was determined to write my own story. Having shifted my focus to staying in India, I began to think about how to create a meaningful life here. So I moved forward, seeking opportunities along the way.

"Dad must be relieved that you're not leaving now. He's been worried about the finances for your plans abroad." Mum said.

"Yes, you all seem happy with this new direction." I replied, though I couldn't hide the unease in my voice. Inside, I was lost. I had no back-up plan, no clear vision of what to do next.

"Being a doctor is a good profession in India." Mum suggested.

"Why?"

"You get respect."

"No one disrespects me now."

"Yes, but this kind of respect comes with money."

"I don't want to work just for money."

"It's a lot of money."

"How much?"

"Become a doctor and we'll find out together."

"Tell me the amount, and I'll think about it."

"Why don't you want to become a doctor, anyway?"

"I don't like what they do."

"What? They treat sick people, they're noble. So many lives would be lost without them. They prevent diseases, they work tirelessly to help others."

"I like that part. But I can't stand being around sick people. If someone sneezes, I avoid talking to them for a day. How can I be a good doctor if I can't even be near patients?"

"People will admire you, too."

"For what?"

"For being a doctor."

"I don't care about what others think."

"Yes, you do." Mum said sharply.

"Yes, I do, but not enough to surround myself with sick people."

"Just start studying for it. Not everyone who wants to be a doctor actually becomes one. Take the subjects, keep your options open. There's no harm in that." Mum said, her voice firm, signalling the end of the conversation.

Later that day, Mum told Dad that I wasn't going to Australia. Surprisingly, he seemed disappointed, too. It almost felt like he wanted me to go abroad after all.

———◦◦◇◦◦———

Time slipped by as I wandered aimlessly, searching for new goals. At 16, I enjoyed the freedom, the sense of being untethered, but I had no clear vision. Every day, my goals shifted. Medicine was out of the question, and neither commerce nor arts felt challenging enough.

"Mummy wants me to take physics, chemistry, maths and biology for 11th and 12th." I told my friend.

"Do you want to be a doctor?" my friend asked.

"Not really. I don't like being around sick people."

"Then why take biology? You're just adding more pressure."

"What's the alternative?"

"Computer science."

"I don't like computers. They make me sleepy. Playing games is fun, but making them sounds boring."

"But you can score, well in computer science."

"Really?"

"Yeah, and it'll boost your overall grades, and that could help you get into better engineering colleges."

"Okay."

I mulled over the decision for days, unsure how to break it to my parents. Every time I imagined the conversation, I knew the response: I had to keep biology to keep the option open of being a doctor. Eventually, two scenarios emerged.

The first was to lie and say I took biology, but I'd be stuck lying after every exam result. I'd need to fabricate stories for the next two years, and it was too risky. So, I chose the second option that just involved one lie.

"Mum, Dad, I couldn't get biology for 11th."

"Why not?"

"The seats filled up quickly."

"Can't they make an exception?" Dad asked.

"If they do it for me, they'd have to do it for everyone."

"So what? If you're the first, who cares about the others?"

"I already asked, but they declined my request."

"You don't know how to ask." Dad said.

"Let me talk to the school tomorrow." Mum suggested.

"There's no point. A lot of us ended up in computer science because we couldn't get into bio." I added, trying to sound convincing.

"All right, give it a try anyway." Mum said.

I retreated to my room, wondering how long I could keep this up. Eventually, I realised there was only one way to put an end to it—I had to tell them the truth.

"Mummy, Papa, I don't want to study bio. I want to be an engineer, so I took computer science." I finally confessed, relieved.

"Okay." they said, though I could sense their disappointment.

———◦◦◇◦◦———

Two years later, I was browsing through a booklet of engineering universities and streams when Dad walked into my room.

"I think you should submit this form." he said.

"Mechanical and electrical engineering look more interesting than the others." I said, without looking up from the booklet.

"Sure, but computer science (CS) is the future. You should choose CS or IT over mechanical or electrical."

"I've studied basic computer science for the past two years, and I didn't enjoy it."

"Studying isn't about enjoyment. It's about securing your future."

"What?"

"You need to study something that will give you stability. Mechanical and electrical engineers work in extreme conditions, but IT engineers get to work comfortably in air-conditioned offices."

"Then I'll choose mechanical engineering."

"Why?"

"I don't like staying indoors."

"IT engineers earn five times more than what you'd make as a mechanical engineer."

"I don't care about the money. I care about doing what I enjoy. I won't enjoy the next four years if I pick what you want."

"But you'll enjoy life after these four years." Dad said.

I glanced at the form, filled with colleges I had no interest in, but there was no point arguing. I grabbed my bike keys and left the house without saying a word.

I reached my friend Swapnil's house, climbed two storeys, and knocked.

"Swapnil, Jaideep's here." his mum called out.

"Come on in." Swapnil said from his room.

"How are you?" I asked.

"Tense." he replied.

"Why?"

"There are too many choices—streams, cities, universities. It's overwhelming."

"Are you thinking of leaving Mumbai?"

"Probably. Pune has a great student scene, and the colleges are good."

"But it's not Mumbai."

"Technically, we don't live in 'real' Mumbai. We're practically in Pune already." he laughed.

"Pune's too cold." I said.

"It's better than the heat here." He changed the subject. "What about you?"

"I'm not so lucky. My dad filled out the entire application for me."

"Good. At least you've got someone to help."

"No, it's not help. It's force. He wants me to take CS or IT, but I want to do mechanical or electrical engineering."

"Why not change it?"

"He already filled in the form on my behalf."

"Then change it before it's too late." Swapnil suggested. "Your dad won't even notice."

"That's risky."

"It's just codes and numbers. No one will know."

I logged into my account on Swapnil's computer and changed my preferences, putting mechanical and electrical at the top. After printing the new version, I submitted it. The relief was immediate, but temporary.

A few days later, Dad discovered I'd changed the preferences. He stormed into my room and slammed the engineering booklet on my desk.

"Who asked you to use your useless brain?" he shouted.

I had prepared for this moment, so I calmly replied, "I can still get into those colleges in the second or third round. For now, I've put better options first."

Dad's anger was palpable. He yelled, but I stayed silent, nodding along, pretending to listen.

———○○◇◇○○———

Weeks later, results day arrived. Early that morning, my phone rang—it was Swapnil.

"Check the results. They're out."

I tried to check, but the website wouldn't load. Hours later, I managed to get through.

"Mummy, I got electrical engineering at Sardar Patel College of Engineering." I said, finally relieved. I'd got my fourth preference—exactly what I wanted.

———○○◇◇○○———

The last three years had flown by in a blur of hostel life, barely scraping through with just enough effort. The hostel was a few kilometres from college, but that didn't stop me from making friends both there and at university, doubling the fun. Every weekend, I'd head home, enjoying the best of both worlds.

The pressure of my final year in engineering weighed heavily on me, making me feel like I was sinking.

Now, in my fourth year, reality was hitting hard. Companies were coming for campus placements, and the previous batch had all secured jobs by the end of May. But this year? A minor recession had swept in, and companies were no longer hiring fresh graduates. The placement coordinator broke the news, and a wave of anxiety rippled through the students. The number of visiting companies dwindled.

In the first two months, I applied to three companies, but didn't clear even the first round. One of the tests had the easiest questions I'd ever seen, but I still failed. My confidence was shattered. Too embarrassed to face my parents, I stopped going home as often, despite Dad sending money to my account like clockwork.

One day, my account ran dry, and I had to ask Dad for more.

"Come home and get the cash." he said, his tone suggesting he also wanted to see me.

Instead, I started taking the same amounts and spent just enough to avoid the embarrassment of facing them every week. By December, the semester break had arrived, and I had no choice but to return home. My private hostel was closed, unlike the college's.

———◦◦◦◦◦◦———

Back home, conversations were tense. "Every day it's costing us 100 rupees. It would've been better if we'd donated that money to the poor and get their blessings." Mum's voice was heavy with disappointment.

When Mum made her comment, I had to admit she had a point. No one was expecting me to get a job that day.

"All right, I'll see you this evening." I said, as I left.

I stopped to pick up Abhinay, my classmate and commute companion, on the way to the station. "Two minutes." he called from his balcony.

"Why so late today?" I asked when he joined me.

"It's cold. I was waiting for the water to heat up."

"I use cold water for showers." I said.

"Why do you do that?"

"Keeps me from catching a cold. The first few seconds are hard, but your body gets used to it."

"Maybe you're right." he shrugged. "Anyway, which company is coming to campus today?"

"I think it's Bajaj, but I don't know if it's Finance or Auto." I said.

He checked his phone. "Bajaj Electricals."

"Okay, let's hope for the best."

By the time we reached the station, I'd told him about my situation. "Thirty companies have come to campus so far. One didn't match my criteria, and I didn't fit the criteria for the rest. I applied to 19 but got rejected in the first round in all except two. One company thought I'd start corruption in their organisation, absurd as that sounds. The other shortlisted me for an interview at 10 a.m., but I didn't get called in until 9:45 that night. I was the last one and was completely exhausted by then."

"What do you think will happen today?" Abhinay asked.

"No pressure today. My parents don't expect me to get placed. I'm just going to enjoy myself."

After a 90-minute train journey and a 20-minute walk, we reached the college. In the placement hall, we met the other candidates, all eager but tense. Five company officials entered, cracking jokes no one laughed at. We were too nervous to respond to their humour. They explained the selection process: two stages—group discussion and a personal interview.

"How many candidates are you looking to hire?" was the first question from a student.

"Two, maybe three max." one of the officials replied. The tension in the room thickened.

I was part of the first group for the discussion. Our topic was *Winning is everything.* I mentally noted my points, ready to start strongly.

Ashish kicked off the discussion: "Winning is everything, and there are many examples to support that."

I jumped in next, feeling positive for the first time in months.

"Before the 1980s, India followed hockey. We won several Olympic golds, but when our performance declined, the country shifted its attention to cricket after winning the 1983 World Cup."

A few classmates nodded in agreement. "Good point, Jaideep." one of them said, and my confidence soared.

But eventually, the conversation drifted away from winning.

"Losing is part of life, too." someone argued, and others followed, discussing the merits of failure. I started to panic, wondering if I'd misunderstood the topic.

But then, one of the company officials interrupted, "Hang on. Jaideep is the only one sticking to the topic—*Winning is everything.*"

Relief washed over me. Not only had I made valid points, but the official addressed me by name. I felt I had a foot in the door.

When the discussion ended, we waited anxiously for the results. After a couple of hours, the placement coordinator read out the names of shortlisted candidates. My name was first on the list!

During the lunch break, a woman came over and called me for the interview.

My nerves kicked in as I walked to the room. I realised I still had my bag with me. I tossed it onto a couch outside the room and took a deep breath before stepping in.

Five interviewers sat across the table. "Don't be nervous. Have some water." one of them said, passing me a glass before the questions began.

"What is the unit of resistance?"

"Ohm."

"In a three-phase system, the voltages are separated by … ?"

"120 degrees."

"Why is alternating current (AC) used for long-distance transmission?"

"Because the voltage is easily changed with a transformer with lower energy loss."

The technical questions continued, and I answered with as much confidence as I could muster.

Then the human resources (HR) person chimed in. "Do you smoke?"

"Yes, sometimes."

"How often?"

"Once or twice a year."

"Just once or twice a year?"

"No, once or twice a month."

"Just once or twice a month?"

"No, once or twice a day."

"Just once or twice a day?"

"Yes, that's it. No more." They laughed.

Then another interviewer asked, "Do you drink?"

"Yes"

"How much?"

"Once or twice a year"

"Just once or twice a year?"

"Yes, only twice a year, after semester results."

"Your marks don't suggest that you should be celebrating."

"Oh no, I do not drink by myself—I'm usually celebrating someone else's good grades or commiserating with someone who failed."

Everyone laughed. I knew I'd lightened the mood.

"Thank you, Jaideep. We'll announce the results at the end of the day."

When the time came, my heart was racing. "We're hiring two candidates today." the representative said. "Sumit Palker." he called out first.

I felt my hopes sink. But then—"Jaideep Padalwar."

Shock and disbelief washed over me as my friends congratulated me and pushed me forward. I walked up to the coordinator, who extended his hand.

"Your offer is conditional." he said.

"What's the condition?"

"You'll need to quit smoking."

"I will. No problem." I blurted, eager to secure the job.

"We have random tests after joining. You'll also need to take one before you start."

"I'm ready."

"Good. Then you're hired." he said, handing me the offer letter.

———◦◦◦◦◦———

It had been a week since I completed my six-month probation at my first job.

"I've got the money, the work experience, and everyone at the office speaks highly of me. I don't know what else I'm supposed to do to get ahead." I said to my childhood friend Ashutosh, catching up with him after work.

"Why do you even want to do more? We're in a much better spot than we were two years ago. Let's just enjoy it." Ashutosh said.

"I want my own office." I said.

"Why?"

"I don't know. I just want it."

"Keep doing good work. One day you'll get there."

"I thought so, too. I even spoke to one of the managers about the career path that leads to having an office." I said, taking a drag on my cigarette.

"Didn't he tell you to quit smoking?" Ashutosh smirked.

"Well, he smokes, too. A lot of people at work do, but they all have their hidden spots around the office. I was shocked when I found out, then I picked up the habit again."

"No medical check-ups?"

"We had one before joining, but nothing since."

"So, what career path did he suggest?" Ashutosh asked.

"He said there are a lot of people who want what I want. Sure, some have similar work experience, but when it comes down to it, the hiring manager will choose the person he likes more."

"So, you've got this in the bag then. You said everyone likes you, and you're good at your job."

"Yeah, but he also mentioned a master's degree might give me an edge over the competition."

"Then do a master's." Ashutosh said, as though applying to university was as simple as ordering a cup of tea.

"It's not that easy."

"Why not?"

"I remember the day I got my campus placement at Bajaj Electricals. I called my dad to tell him, and I've never heard him so happy. Mum spread the news to the entire building. I got congratulated by everyone as I climbed the stairs to our flat. Even my brother, Amar, was over the moon—he bought sweets to celebrate. It was like I made everyone proud for the first time. And then, as soon as I landed the job, Dad bought an apartment in my name, tying me down with financial responsibilities to make sure I settled."

"So, what's the problem?"

"If I tell them now that I want to quit my job and do an MBA, it'll come as a huge shock. They won't be happy."

"Then suggest it gradually. Gauge their reaction."

"I can't."

"Why not?"

"I don't have the guts."

"Then act like a coward." Ashutosh grinned, knowing exactly how to push my buttons.

"How?"

"Do everything behind their backs, and when it's time to tell them, tell them. That way, if you fail, no one knows."

"I could try that ... But what do I need to do to get into an MBA program?"

"You'll probably need to take some exams, like CAT (Common Admission Test)."

"That's tough. People study for years to crack those exams. The longer I work, the less motivated I feel to hit the books again."

"Nothing good comes easy." he said, grinning.

"Shut up." I said, giving him a shove.

"So, what's your plan?"

"My first six months at work were just training. For the first month, they introduced us to all the business units. After that, they assigned me to the Luminaire Business Unit. For the next month, I rotated through each department, and then they stuck me in marketing. It seemed interesting at first, but both my manager and his boss were new too, so they were still learning the ropes. I spent the entire month doing nothing. I was bored out of my mind. That's when I started thinking about a master's in illumination engineering. I Googled it, and Australia kept popping up as a good place to study."

"What about safety?"

"According to Google, it's not such a problem anymore. The last major incident was five years ago, and things have improved since. That research sparked my interest in Australia again. Apparently, they're looking for electrical engineers, especially with their focus on renewable energy. There are job opportunities there, too."

Ashutosh and I sat quietly for a while, mulling over my situation. After a few minutes, he said, "Talk to Nikhil. He's planning to go to the U.S. for his master's."

"I don't have that kind of money." I said, shaking my head.

"The tuition fees are similar, but it's the living expenses that add up. You can cover those with part-time jobs."

"How do you know all this?"

"I listen to people."

"Are you planning to go yourself?"

"Definitely not. I just remember what Nikhil said, the last time we met."

"All right, let's call him."

Ashutosh dialled Nikhil's number and handed me his phone.

"Hello?"

"Hi Nikhil, it's Jaideep. Where are you?" I asked.

"At home."

"Want to meet up?"

"Why?"

"How about I tell you when I see you? I'm with Ashutosh. We're at the tea stall near Chopstix."

"All right, I'll be there in ten."

"He's on his way." I told Ashutosh, lighting another cigarette. Five minutes later, Nikhil arrived.

"Hey." he said, shaking our hands. "What's going on?"

"We need to ask you about doing a master's abroad." I said.

"I can answer some questions, but I'm still figuring it out myself."

"How much does it cost?" Ashutosh asked.

"Around AU$100,000 or 50 lakhs for a two-year program."

"Is it worth it?" Ashutosh asked.

"Yes. In the U.S., people can earn that much in a year."

"Fifty lakhs in one year?" We were both stunned.

"So, you could pay off the loan in a couple of years." I said.

"Yeah, but it depends on post-graduation expenses. I only know the costs while studying."

"What's the process?" I asked.

"You take two exams: GRE (Graduate Record Examinations) or GMAT (Graduate Management Aptitude Test) for aptitude, and TOEFL (Test of English as a Foreign Language) for English. Then, based on your scores, you apply to universities. Once you get an offer, you pay the fees and start the visa process."

"And Australia? Is it the same?" I asked.

"It should be."

"Where do I start?"

"Go to a counsellor. They can guide you and coordinate with universities."

"Or I could just call up agencies and see who's the most helpful." I said.

"That works, too. But check exam dates; they fill up fast."

"All right, I'll start tomorrow. I'm done thinking for today. I'm starving." I said. We parted ways, but I kept mulling over my plan that night. Eventually, I decided to call a counsellor.

I got home, my mind so heavy. that I couldn't muster the courage to tell my parents about my plan. Besides, it didn't make sense to say anything yet. I had no concrete steps in place, just vague ideas. So, I decided to keep it to myself for now.

That night, I stayed up, thinking of how to start exploring opportunities in Australia. The key, I figured, was asking the right questions. After speaking to a few friends, many suggested I reach out to Institute of Management and Foreign Studies (IMFS), an agency that specialised in helping students go abroad. A friend gave me their contact, and the next morning, I decided to call.

"Hello?" A man with a deep voice answered. "This is Oliver from IMFS. How can I help you?"

"Hi, I'm Jaideep." I began, trying to sound confident. "A friend of mine recommended you. I'm looking into studying in Australia, and I was wondering if you could assist with that."

"You've come to the right place." he said smoothly, and I immediately felt wary of his rehearsed sales pitch.

"Uh-huh." I replied, a bit dubious now.

"Tell me about yourself." he said, his tone shifting to casual, almost conversational.

"What would you like to know?"

"Well, for starters, your educational background."

"I did my bachelor's in electrical engineering at Sardar Patel College of Engineering, Andheri."

"Great college." Oliver said quickly. "I've been there a few times. Good campus."

"Yes, it is." I agreed.

"When did you graduate?"

"May 2013."

"And are you working now?"

"Yes, I'm working at Bajaj Electricals in the supply chain department. It's been six months."

"Six months? That's a good start. Now, listen to me carefully. You've probably done some research already."

"I have, yes."

"Then you'd likely know that electrical engineers are in high demand in Australia. And with Australia being an importing country, supply chain management is crucial. With your education and a couple more years of experience, you'll have a solid foundation to make the move. You could find roles in either engineering or management."

"I'm actually more interested in management. I'm getting tired of the technical side."

"Then you've got two great options: an MBA or a master's in engineering management."

"Both sound good. Can you walk me through them?"

"Of course." he said, his tone professional again. "Where do you live?"

"Panvel."

"Perfect. We have an office in Vashi, near the station. We can meet there, even on the weekend."

"Sounds good. I can come this weekend."

"Is this number the best way to reach you?"

"Yes, it is."

"Great. I'll send you our address and confirm the appointment via text."

"Okay, see you then." I hung up, feeling a little more confident, but still cautious.

The next morning, Saturday, I woke up to the sound of a truck's horn blaring outside. I began thinking about how to explain leaving the house on a weekend without raising a lot of questions. After running through a few scenarios, I landed on the least problematic one.

"Mummy, I need to go to the office for a couple of hours." I said casually over breakfast.

"On a Saturday?" she asked, eyebrows raised.

"Yeah, work can pop up anytime." I shrugged.

"Why can't you do it from home?"

"Everyone's going in. We need to finalise some things."

She paused for a moment. "Okay. What time are you leaving?"

"Around 10."

"And when will you be back?"

"In three hours. Thirty minutes to get there, two hours of work, and then 30 minutes back."

"All right, I'll make breakfast for you before you go."

"Thanks." I said, thinking I had pulled off the lie pretty well. I got ready, ate quickly, and left the house.

Little did I know that one small step out the door would lead to a journey that would take me many miles from home.

UNKNOWNS AND UNCERTAINTIES

"Good morning! This is Jaideep. I applied for my Australian student visa. Can you please provide an update on my application?" I asked the Australian Visa Authority.

"Hello, when did you apply for it?" the woman on the other end asked.

"Three weeks ago." I replied.

"Please check the Australian Visa website for the processing timelines. All student visa applications can take up to three months to process."

"But I've already booked my flight for July 18, and that's only eight days away." I said, my voice tightening with anxiety.

"We didn't ask you to book your flight." she said. "You should have checked the processing times before booking. Check your visa status in another two months."

I paused, frustrated. "Okay, but is there any way you could expedite my application?"

"We cannot prioritise it before the standard timeline." she said.

My heart sank. I felt like my entire body had gone numb. My mind was racing, but I couldn't find the words to respond. Anger surged in me. I wanted to scream at her to do her job better or bribe her to push my application forward. But I knew that would only make things worse. I reminded myself that life only gives us challenges we can overcome.

"Okay, thank you." I muttered.

I started pacing the room, biting my nails, my mind spinning with panic. Everything felt out of control. I couldn't think of a single way to get my visa faster. After a few minutes, I grabbed my phone and dialled a friend's number.

"Hello, Mihir. I'm screwed. Let's catch up. Can I come around?" I said, my voice trembling.

"Okay. See you soon." he replied.

I started walking towards the front door, trying to avoid eye contact with Mum and Amar, sitting in the living room. By the time I reached the door, I still hadn't come up with anything convincing.

"Mummy, I'll be back soon." I said, hastily slipping out the door and rushing down the stairs. I grabbed my bike and rode to Mihir's place, desperate to unload the stress of my conversation with the visa officer.

When I arrived, Mihir was waiting outside. "What's wrong? You look so tense!"

"I quit my job ten days ago because I thought I'd get my visa in time and have a chance to spend some time with my family before leaving for Australia. But now the visa official says it'll take another two months. I'll miss the winter intake! How am I supposed to tell my parents? Should I call my ex-boss and beg for my job back? I don't know what to do …"

"Calm down! Just take some time and tell your parents when you're ready."

Mihir and I had known each other since school, and he understood when I needed to talk and when I needed quiet. His silence was comforting.

"I've been at this for so long, Mihir. Eighteen months of preparing and planning, and if this doesn't work out, I'll lose confidence in myself. Everyone will." I said.

Mihir just nodded, letting me speak.

"I still remember my first visit to the counsellor." I continued. "Feels like forever ago. The counsellor told me to take the GRE and TOEFL, so I woke up at 4 a.m. every day to study for two hours. Then I'd go to the gym for half an hour to clear my head, then off to work. I'd come home at 8 p.m., eat, sleep, and do it all again the next day."

"Yes. Very good." Mihir said.

"And the best part?" I added, trying to make the conversation more engaging.

"What's that?" Mihir asked.

"I didn't even need the GRE for this program." I said with a half-smile.

"Which course did you finally settle on? You had so many offers I lost track."

"That's a whole fiasco in itself." I sighed.

"Why?"

"I was fixated on Sydney. I only wanted universities with technology or engineering in the name. University of Technology Sydney was my top choice."

"You got an offer from them, right? So why did you end up choosing Melbourne?"

"I got three offers, actually." I explained. "The first was a master's in engineering management, and I was thrilled at first. It was exactly what I wanted! But then I realised it was only a one-year course. It sounded great initially—less time, less money—but when I called my agent, he said that a one-year course doesn't qualify you for a post-study work visa. No scope for staying longer or working after graduation."

"What did you say then?"

"I asked the counsellor why he applied for that course in the first place!" I said, exasperated. "Then I told him to change my application for a two-year course to master's in engineering management and another in electrical engineering. But he messed it up again. I ended up with offers for engineering management and ... computer engineering."

"Computer engineering?" Mihir raised an eyebrow.

"Yeah, I don't know anything about computers! I had to ask him to apply again for electrical engineering. Somehow, I ended up with a third offer—this time for engineering management and IT. I felt like I was never going to get what I wanted."

"Man, that sounds rough."

"Eventually, my application got transferred to the Delhi office after my agent Oliver left. The new agent was more helpful and finally got me an offer for a two-year course at RMIT (university) in Melbourne. I Googled the university, saw it had a good reputation, and decided to accept."

"So, it worked out in the end?"

"Sort of. I got the offer from RMIT, but when it came time to apply for an education loan, no bank wanted to back me without collateral. I tried pitching them my plans, but they wouldn't budge. I had to involve my parents, which I was dreading."

"How did that go?"

"I don't even remember the exact moment. We were watching TV as a family, and out of nowhere, I just blurted, 'Papa, I want to go to Australia for my master's. I've been accepted at a university in Melbourne, and I need a loan for AU$60,000 i.e.

approximately 30 lakhs. I've tried applying myself, but they need your support'."

"Oh, wow. What did your dad say?"

"The room went dead silent. I didn't stick around to find out. I got up and locked myself in my room right after saying it. I'm not sure if it was the money or the idea of me leaving that shocked them. Maybe both."

Mihir nodded thoughtfully. "That must've been tough for them."

"Yeah, but in the end, he agreed. The loan terms weren't great—I'll have to start paying interest while I'm still studying—but at least it's sorted. Now, the only thing left is the visa, and I'm praying I get it soon."

After venting, I felt a little more relaxed. Mihir and I joked about random things, our laughter dissolving the tension. But even after the laughs, the worry still lingered in the back of my mind.

When I got home, I went straight to my room, avoiding Mum and Amar. I lay on my bed, staring at the ceiling, thinking about how to tell my mum that I might not be going to Australia after all. All that money spent on university fees ... wasted. And what if I can't get my job back?

As these thoughts weighed on me, my phone pinged. I absentmindedly checked the notification, expecting spam. But then I saw it—a Gmail notification that read: "[SPAM] Visa Grant Notification."

I froze. Could it really be? I sprang upright, ignoring the "[SPAM]" in the email subject, and opened the message. As I waited for it to load, my heart raced. It was the Visa Grant Notice. I read every word slowly, carefully dissecting the entire message. After what felt like an eternity, I finally finished reading it, closed my eyes and thanked God. A wave of relief washed over me. I took a deep breath, exhaled heavily, and went to find my mum.

"Mummy, I got my visa!" I said, unable to hide my excitement.

"Very good!" Her face lit up. "When are you leaving?"

"In ten days."

We celebrated together, waiting for Dad to return from work so we could share the news with him. Meanwhile, Amar and I watched *The Big Bang Theory*, trying to enjoy the moment despite the whirlwind of things still left to do. I began searching for accommodation in Melbourne but quickly found myself overwhelmed by all the options. I decided to ask my counsellor for advice.

I called the agent who had connected me with the universities. After a few rings, she answered.

"Hi Bhumika, it's Jaideep. I got my visa!"

"Congratulations, Jaideep!"

"I've been going through your checklist and trying to gather everything I need before leaving. I wanted to ask—do you know if there's anyone else heading to Melbourne from India? It would be great to connect with someone before I go."

"Let me check our database." After a brief pause, she returned with, "Unfortunately, you're the only student going to Melbourne this year. Most others are heading to Sydney."

A chill went down my spine, thinking about navigating a foreign country when I didn't yet speak fluent English. But I quickly shook off the nerves and resumed my search for accommodation. Melbourne was more expensive than I'd expected, and I knew I needed to find something affordable. Desperate, I reached out to random people on Facebook for advice. One kind stranger recommended checking out Gumtree and Flat-mates.com.

I first tried Gumtree, but the sheer number of listings left me confused. Then, I moved to Flatmates. I liked the platform's layout and quickly found a place that caught my eye—a shared apartment near RMIT, where I'd be studying. The listing said it had four rooms and was located in the heart of the city, close to RMIT and the University of Melbourne. It sounded perfect. The property manager's name was Jack, so I gave him a call.

"Hey Jack, good morning! This is Jaideep from Mumbai, India. I'm moving to Melbourne in a few days and found your listing on Flatmates. Do you still have space available?"

"Hi! Sorry, what was your name again?" Jack asked.

"Jaideep. J-A-I-D-E-E-P. I'm starting my master's at RMIT soon and was wondering if your place would be a good fit. What's the rent, and is there still room for one person?"

"Yes, we've got space, and it's close to RMIT. Rent is AU$600 a month."

I quickly did the maths—about INR30,000—less than some places in Mumbai. It seemed like a great deal, so I decided to book it for a month.

"That sounds perfect. I'd like to go ahead and book it."

"Great! We'll need a deposit—two weeks' rent, which is AU$300."

"All right. I'll send the payment after the call. How far is the university?"

"Not far. Some RMIT buildings are nearby, and the rest are accessible via free trams in the CBD."

"That's fantastic. How much notice do I need to give before moving out?"

"Two weeks' notice is required. You can either pay for the last two weeks upfront or not pay for them if you're leaving."

"Sounds good. I'll send over the payment details shortly."

After we hung up, I looked at other options, but nothing matched Jack's place for price or convenience. I emailed him the deposit and filled out the necessary paperwork. With accommodation sorted, I felt one step closer to the reality of moving.

While we were waiting for Dad, we saw his company car pull up. As he entered the house, he noticed the strange, expectant way we were all looking at him.

"Why are you all staring at me like that?" he asked. "It's been a long day of travel—don't keep me in suspense!"

"Dada got his visa!" Amar announced, using the respectful term for elder brother.

"That's wonderful." Dad said with a smile, but I could see the emotion behind his eyes. The joy of his son achieving a big milestone was tempered by the reality of me leaving soon. It was a bittersweet moment. I could sense his pride, but I knew it was hard for him to watch me go.

Dad had always hoped his sons would go abroad to work and earn a good living, not necessarily to invest in an expensive education. I knew that my plan of studying overseas, incurring debt and starting from scratch, was the opposite of what he'd envisioned. It was a financial risk for an average Indian family like ours, one that could take years—if not decades—to recover from.

But despite these concerns, he swallowed his worries, smiled and supported my decision.

—◦◦◦◦◦—

"When are you leaving?" my brother asked, shaking me awake next morning. "In nine days, and I've got so much to do." I replied groggily.

"Flight tickets are booked, right?"

"Yep."

"So, what's left?"

"Shopping." I said, raising my thumb.

"People usually buy things after they arrive. You don't need to buy too much here."

"But if I buy everything here, Dad will pay for it. If I wait until I get there, I'll have to pay myself." I said, and we both laughed.

I raised my index finger next. "Haircut."

"You just got one last week."

"My friend told me it's expensive to cut hair over there. So, I'm thinking of cutting it really short before I leave. That way, I won't need another haircut for two months. Plus, I don't know where to get one there."

"Makes sense."

Next, I added my middle finger to the count. "Currency conversion."

"How much do you have to convert?"

"After booking flights, accommodation and accounting for other expenses, I've got around two lakhs left."

"How much is that in Australian dollars?"

"Four thousand dollars."

"Are you carrying cash or keeping it in your account?"

"Some cash."

"How much?"

"I'm thinking of taking 25,000 rupees in cash and leaving the rest in the account."

"Okay, how much is that in Australian dollars?"

"Only 500."

"That's nothing."

"Well, it's my savings, so don't talk about it like that!"

"All right, all right. Anything else?"

"Yeah, one more thing." I lifted my fourth finger. "Leather jacket."

"Why?"

"Jayesh said Australia can get pretty cold, and a leather jacket not only helps with the cold but looks good, too."

"How cold does it get in Melbourne?"

"Around five degrees."

"And you think a leather jacket will be enough?"

"I hope so. I've got no other idea how I'm going to survive in that cold."

"Where are you planning to get it?"

"Dharavi. It's the biggest slum in Asia, but they've got the best-quality leather products at cheap prices. I'm after a jacket and maybe a belt."

"I hope that's it then. Nothing more to buy, right?"

"There's one last thing."

Amar looked at me, slightly anxious, probably wondering what else I needed before leaving. After a pause, he asked, "What is it?"

"This list from the counsellor." I handed it to him. He looked at it in disbelief and started reading aloud.

"Things to carry in hand luggage, up to 7 kg permitted:

- passport
- visa grant notification
- additional institution documents
- offer letter
- fee receipt
- airport pickup confirmation
- accommodation address

- air tickets
- travel insurance
- academic mark sheets
- certificates
- marriage certificate (if spouse is travelling)
- cash/travellers cheques."

He took a deep breath before continuing.
"Main luggage:

- 15 passport-sized photos
- writing pads
- notebooks
- diary
- pens
- pencils
- highlighters
- stapler
- paper punch
- paper clips
- calculator
- USB stick
- textbook
- three sets of formal wear for presentations or important functions
- clothes according to weather
- casual clothes for the immediate season."

Then he got to the kitchen items, which were marked as very important.

- "Pressure cooker (small one, keep it open, cover separately)
- plates
- mugs (avoid glass items)
- spoons, and other useful utensils
- cooking masalas, all spices sealed properly—open items won't pass customs
- Maggi/noodles—bring a few packs, they're useful."

He continued reading the list, now on to personal items.

- "Two sets of bed linen
- spare spectacles and contact lenses
- prescriptions for any regular medications
- photographs of family and friends (helpful when feeling low or homesick)
- towels
- soap
- toothpaste (expensive there)
- toothbrushes, and other basics."

Finally, he got to electrical appliances, also marked as important.

- "Iron
- hairdryer
- laptop

- iPod
- camera with charger
- electric plug with three flat pins and an adapter."

Amar handed the list back to me, exhausted. "Last thing on the list is academic books."

We had breakfast, watched a movie at home, and then, out of nowhere, he asked the toughest question of the day.

"How will you handle the finances?"

"I'll get a part-time job once I'm there." I said, hoping to sound more confident than I felt.

"Okay, have you done some research?"

"Yeah, I've looked into it."

"And?"

"Who are you? Dad?" I teased.

"No, I just want to know how much you're going to spend and how much you'll leave for me!"

"Well, I'm planning to work in a restaurant. That'll help me earn money and cover food expenses."

"Why don't you learn to cook yourself?"

"Mum taught me a few things: dry potato curry, bread with butter, and cauliflower curry."

"Only three dishes?"

"Yeah, I'll live on those until I learn more. But if I get a job at a restaurant, I won't need to cook."

I sounded casual, but deep down, I was nervous about how it would all work out.

"Now stop asking questions and let's relax for a while." I changed the subject, eager to just spend time with him.

———∞∞∞———

"Are any of your friends coming with us to drop you off at the airport?" my mum asked when I woke up to get ready for my departure.

"Yes, Jayesh and Tushar said they'd come."

"It's raining heavily, and it's very early. Get confirmation from them so we can pick them up on our way to the airport." Dad said.

"Okay, I'll call them now."

I dialled Jayesh. "Hello, Jayesh. Are you still coming to the airport?"

"Yes, I'm getting up now."

"Good."

"At what time are we leaving?" he asked.

"Our flight is at 9:30 a.m. The airline recommends arriving three hours early." I replied.

"So, we need to be there by 6:30 then." he calculated.

"Exactly. So, we should leave by 5:00 a.m. to make sure we get there on time. Hopefully, the rain won't cause too much traffic."

"It's too early for heavy traffic. We should reach there on time."

"Okay. Will you call Tushar and confirm with him as well? Tell him to be ready, or we'll have to leave without him." I said, laughing.

A while later, Jayesh texted that Tushar would be ready.

"Both of them are set." I told Dad while he was calling the driver to confirm he was on schedule.

"The driver will be on time, too. Amar is still sleeping. Let him rest." Dad said.

"Why not wake him up?" I asked.

"No, don't." Mum said.

"Why not?" I persisted.

"He's very unhappy about your departure. He's been quite depressed the last few days."

"Let me spend a bit more time with him." I said.

"There's no time for that. Get ready first. Once you're ready, we'll wake him up." Dad said.

By the time I was dressed, Amar was already up and waiting for me. As soon as I came out, he hugged me tightly.

I returned the hug and said, "Don't worry. I am not leaving you. I'm only going far away, physically, but you will always be my dear brother. No one ever can take your place. I'll come back some day especially to see you. We'll have fun together once we both are successful. Meanwhile, study hard and prepare to become a big figure in the future. I won't be here to disturb you while you study." I smiled through my teary eyes. "Cheer up now. Get ready. I'm running late. I have a plane to catch."

Amar understood and quickly got ready. While he was finishing up, I took a moment to pray for protection, and enjoyed a final breakfast made by Mum. I savoured every bite, knowing it would be a long time before I tasted her cooking again.

"Driver's here." Dad said, taking the luggage downstairs.

I grabbed my backpack, checked for my passport, visa copy, university enrolment confirmation and accommodation details. Satisfied, I picked up my luggage and started walking downstairs. Amar followed me, and Mum was the last one out, locking the door behind us.

I called Tushar to confirm he was ready. He was, and he said he'd get Jayesh to come downstairs as well. The driver helped us load the luggage into the car. I opened the front door and began to climb in.

"I'll sit in the front." Dad said. "You sit in the middle with Amar and Mum."

"No, I'll sit in the front so I can see everyone when I turn around." I said, jumping in.

Mum, Dad and Amar took the middle row, and we left the back row seats for my friends. We picked them up and crossed the bridge, leaving the suburb where I'd spent my childhood. I knew every street, had watched it evolve from a village to a town, and heard friends from Mumbai refer to it as a resting place on their way to Pune.

We chatted during the drive. After an hour, we arrived at the airport. Only I could enter, due to strict Mumbai airport regulations.

I said goodbye, hugging Mum, Dad, Amar, Jayesh and Tushar. With a heavy heart and a tinge of anxiety, I walked towards the gate. I placed my luggage on the scale at the check-in booth and saw it was three kilos over the limit.

"Passport, flight ticket, and visa, please." the woman at the counter requested, not even glancing at the scale.

I handed her my documents, hoping she wouldn't notice the extra weight. I considered what I might be able to offload to my parents, who were waiting to wave me goodbye.

She glanced at the scale and said, "Are you a student?"

"Yes."

"For first-timers, we can provide additional luggage at no extra cost. Just be sure to adhere to the weight limits next time."

"Yes, I will." I replied with a relieved smile.

"Your flight is at gate 17. Proceed through security over there." she directed, pointing to my right.

"Thank you." I said, looking back at my family and friends through the glass. I smiled, waved, and gave them a thumbs-up to let them know everything was fine.

With a heavy heart and teary eyes, I walked towards the security gates. My legs felt like they wanted to turn back, and my hands ached to hold them tightly. I fought the urge to turn around, knowing it would only make it harder. I was scared—wondering if Australia would accept me, if I would make friends, and how I would handle everything on my own.

But as my brain took over, it reminded me that I'd made it this far. I *had* to make it big in Australia. This was my first flight, my first time at an airport. The news always focused on the rare disasters, not the everyday success stories. So, I pushed aside my fears and focused on the journey ahead.

A 14-hour journey awaited me, not just a change of countries but a complete shift in my world. I faced strangers speaking a language I struggled with, and I dreaded the thought of cooking for myself. I wished someone could be by my side, but none of my friends could join me.

I passed through security without issues and reached gate 17. I called Dad, "Hello, I've reached the gate, and everything went smoothly."

He sounded relieved. "Good. How was immigration?"

"It'll be in Delhi. This flight is domestic. The international leg starts from Delhi."

"Okay. Call us when you reach Delhi."

"Yes, I will. Where are you now?"

"Almost an hour away from home. There's heavy traffic."

"All right. Bye."

"Bye!" I hung up, ready to face the long journey ahead.

———∞◇◇∞———

I had to wait an hour and a half for the boarding call. To pass the time, my first thought was to have a smoke. I immediately searched for a smoking area and found one after a short walk. As I smoked, I focused on the positives—how I was getting closer to my dream. The nervousness and anxiety started to melt away, replaced by a sense of happiness. I was one big step closer to the future I'd been imagining.

After about half an hour of daydreaming, I wandered to a nearby newspaper stand and grabbed a paper to catch up on the latest news. Before long, the boarding call for my domestic flight was announced. I called my parents to let them know.

As usual, I was among the first in line, so I boarded early and took my window seat. I was looking forward to the journey, eager to catch a view of the city I loved. Once the plane filled up and the cabin crew went through their safety instructions, we took off.

From above, Mumbai looked magical—this city that would forever be a part of me. I felt a pang of homesickness creeping in, but just as I started to reflect on leaving my comfort zone, the plane hit a patch of turbulence.

My thoughts of home were quickly replaced by a surge of fear. I gripped the armrests and began silently chanting every god's name I could remember. Sometime later, the pilot's voice crackled through the speakers.

"Attention, passengers. We are unable to land at this time. We are awaiting clearance from the airport authorities. We will update you shortly."

My stomach dropped. I flagged down a flight attendant.

"Excuse me, the flight's delayed, but I have a connecting flight to Melbourne. What should I do?" I asked, trying to keep calm.

"When is your next flight?" she asked.

"In an hour."

"That's a bit tight, but don't worry. For close connections like this, the airline will make arrangements."

"What kind of arrangements?"

"They'll have someone waiting for you at the gate to help you get to your next flight quickly."

"So I'll make it?"

"Yes, the airline will take care of it." she told me before moving on.

Not long after, the pilot announced, "Cabin crew, prepare for landing."

Relief washed over me, and I braced myself for touchdown. We finally landed in Delhi, but the delay had eaten into my layover time—I had only 40 minutes left. The crew informed us that an airport official would guide passengers with tight connections to their gates.

I hurried off the plane and quickly found the official, who was leading a small group of us to our next flights. As we sped through the terminal, I called my mum.

"Hey, I've reached Delhi." I said, slightly out of breath.

"Why are you late? Are you going to miss your flight?" she asked, clearly worried.

"No, no, everything's fine. The airport has it under control—they're helping us get to our connecting flights."

"Okay, just let us know when you board."

"I will, don't worry."

I reached security, where I quickly emptied my pockets and placed my belongings in the tray. After the screening, I followed the official towards immigration.

"Where are you flying to?" the immigration officer asked, giving me a stern look.

"Melbourne." I replied, trying to stay calm.

"For what purpose?"

"Tertiary study. For a master's in engineering."

"Do you have a letter from the university?"

"Yes, from the Royal Melbourne Institute of Technology." I said, pulling out the documents from my backpack and handing them over. The officer glanced through everything, stamped my passport, and waved me through.

"Thanks!" I said.

As I approached the departure gate, I noticed an elderly woman struggling with her luggage. She seemed to be headed for the same flight. I offered to help and carried her bags to the plane, handing them to the flight attendant, who stowed them above her seat. Then I relaxed in my window seat, texted my mum to let her know I'd boarded, and settled in for the long journey ahead.

This was my first international flight, and the excitement was mixed with a bit of nervousness. I'd heard about the perks of international travel—meals, drinks and the chance to experience something new. As I gazed out the window, watching planes take off, I started imagining the stories of the people aboard them— some leaving families behind, others reuniting, some travelling for work and others for pleasure. A smile crept across my face as I thought about how this flight was the beginning of a new chapter for me.

Soon, the flight attendants instructed us to fasten our seat-belts. I gripped the armrests again as the plane accelerated down the runway. I could feel the plane lifting off, and the sensation of gravity pressing against me was overwhelming. My heart raced as I watched the ground get farther and farther away. I silently chanted "Ram, Ram, Ram." praying for a smooth journey.

Once we were in the air and I'd calmed down, I started watching a movie to distract myself. After about an hour, boredom set in. I longed to stretch my legs but didn't want to disturb the people in the middle and aisle seats. So, I stayed put, eagerly waiting for the drinks to be served. When the flight attendant finally came around, I asked for a whiskey and Coke. Shortly after, lunch was served, and I ate, drank and drifted off to sleep.

The day had been long, and sleep came easily. For the next several hours I alternated between watching movies, eating and dozing off. I watched the flight path on the screen in front of me and thought about how vast the world seemed. The plane crossed the Bay of Bengal, and I found myself again chanting "Ram, Ram, Ram" as irrational fears of plane mishaps crept into my mind.

At some point, I got up to stretch and walk around the cabin. I saw someone standing near the door, which inspired me to do the same. After a while, I returned to my seat and continued to watch the flight path. The plane was now over Malaysia—halfway there. I sighed, bored and exhausted, and closed my eyes, imagining what I'd do after landing.

After a short nap, I was pleasantly surprised to see we'd reached the Australian mainland, but realised my destination was still four hours away. When the plane began its descent into Melbourne, the sight filled me with a mix of relief and anticipation. The plane touched down at 6 a.m. and I immediately called home.

"Mum, I've landed in Melbourne!" my voice brimming with excitement.

"How was the flight?" she asked.

"It was good, just long and boring. I mostly ate and slept."

"All right, take care and call me when you reach your place." she said.

I followed the crowd, and quickly cleared immigration. I'd filled out an arrival card on the plane, marking "Yes" for carrying more than 50 cigarettes. I was pulled aside for a baggage check, and my heart raced again—would they send me back for something as silly as this?

Fortunately, they searched everything except the backpack where I'd stored my duty-free cigarettes.

As I stepped out of the airport, I was conscious of entering a new phase of life, with hopes that one day my family would forgive me for leaving them behind.

It was 7 a.m. on a Saturday, still pitch dark and so cold that my palms had gone numb. My heartbeat pulsed in my ears, fast and loud. I stood still for a few seconds, stomach churning, eyes shut, trying to steady my excited mind.

Before leaving India, I'd bought a leather jacket, thinking it would be enough for extreme cold—my idea of "extreme" being anything below five degrees Celsius. But it was two degrees. My bones felt frozen. All I wanted was to get to my accommodation and sleep. I called a taxi.

The driver turned out to be Indian, and I thanked my stars. It felt like everything was going better than expected since landing. Relieved, I decided to ask as many questions as I could in Hindi, my comfort language.

After loading my bags into the boot, I sat diagonally behind the driver to have a better conversation angle. I mentally rehearsed the questions I planned to ask, feeling confident I wouldn't need to write anything down.

"Hello, good morning! How are you?" the driver asked, surprising me with his cheerful tone.

"Good morning! I'm good. How are you?"

"All good! Where are you headed?"

"277 Queensberry Street." I replied, my accent making it clear I wasn't too comfortable speaking English. The driver noticed.

"You're from India? Do you speak Hindi?" he asked.

"*Haan.*" I responded, immediately feeling at ease.

I wasted no time. "Is it always this cold, or is today an exception?"

"Melbourne is always cold, and this is the peak of winter. It'll get even colder in the coming days."

"Great." I said, eyebrows raised. I had no idea how I'd survive my first outing. "How do people handle this weather?"

"Every house has heaters. They'll keep you warm indoors." he said, pausing for a moment.

"And outdoors?"

"Wear proper clothes for the cold."

"Where can I get those at a good price?"

"Kmart and Target. They have affordable options."

"Thanks. And where do people buy daily essentials around here?"

"There are big supermarkets like Coles, Woolworths and Aldi. You'll find everything you need there."

"Where are they located?"

"If they're not on every street, they're close enough." he said, laughing. I smiled along, not quite understanding what was funny.

"Is public transport good here?" I asked.

"Melbourne's CBD is in a free-tram zone, so you can travel around the city centre without paying. What university are you attending?"

"RMIT."

"Great! You'll have no trouble getting there."

We filled the 25-minute drive from the airport with casual conversation. I watched the scenery change from houses to city buildings and bridges. Despite the early hour, the streets were buzzing with people.

"It's so nice to see so many people out and about this early on a Saturday." I said.

The driver chuckled. "It's not Saturday morning for them— it's still Friday night."

"But it's 7:30 a.m.." I said, confused.

"You'll get used to city life soon enough. You'll see I'm right."

"Okay." I said. "Only time will tell."

"Hmm. We're almost there."

"Thanks. Let me call my contact." I dialled Jack, but there was no answer. A wave of panic hit me. "They're not answering! What if I've been scammed?" I asked the driver, my voice shaky.

"Relax. He's probably partying or sleeping. It's still early for a Saturday."

We turned left onto Elizabeth Street and arrived at 277 Queensberry. I looked around, feeling uneasy. The building didn't look like somewhere I could live. The driver was busy unloading my luggage. When he was done, he stood beside me.

"Here we are. Enjoy your time. If you need anything, call me." He handed me his card.

"Where is this place?" I asked, glancing around.

"This is it." he said, pointing at a two-storey brick building with large glass windows. Through them, I saw work desks that made it look like an office. To the far right was a small door.

"What kind of place is this?" I asked, feeling my nerves rising.

"People live in places like this in the city. Where did you find it?"

"Flatmates."

"Then it's legit. Don't worry."

"But Jack isn't answering."

"Try again." the driver suggested, standing beside me. He wasn't going to leave me stranded.

Once more it went straight to voicemail. I shook my head, disappointed.

"Do you have another contact for this place?" the driver asked.

"I do, actually." I called, but again it went to voicemail. "No answer." I muttered.

The driver frowned. "Now it's starting to seem like a scam. If you told Jack what time you'd arrive, he should be here. If not, someone should be helping you out. This doesn't look right." He started typing a message on his phone. "I've asked in my group if anyone has accommodation available. Let's wait a bit."

"But I've already paid a deposit here." I said, worried.

"We'll think about that later. Here, Indians help each other. Everyone knows it's tough to survive in a new country."

"What do you mean by *survive*?" I asked.

"You'll understand soon enough. Australia looks shiny from India, but life here is harder. The problems are bigger."

Just then, his phone pinged. "One of my friends knows a place in a nearby suburb. Let's wait a bit and see."

Before I could respond, my phone rang. The sound was the most comforting thing I'd heard in a while. I answered immediately.

"Hello, who's this?" a voice asked.

"Hi, I'm Jaideep. I got your number from Jack. I've booked accommodation at 277 Queensberry, but I can't get in. Can you help?"

"Give me five minutes. I'll be right down."

"Thank you." I said, relief flooding through me. I turned to the driver and expressed my gratitude. He smiled and waited with me until the door opened, and I was greeted with a simple "Come in."

I thanked the driver one last time with a nod. Overwhelmed by it all—the new country, the unfamiliar place, and the realisation that there was no going back—I stepped inside.

It hit me then: I was alone. No more friends, no brother to share the moment with, no mother's comforting lap, no father's stern but loving criticism. It was time to begin a new life, a new journey.

STRANGER
IN A STRANGE LAND

I stepped inside, and as the door clicked shut behind me, the lights flickered on. I was impressed. A motion sensor in a personal house? I always thought that was a luxury only found in commercial buildings. Maybe not in India, I thought. Perhaps in Australia, people use them in their homes, too.

"That's impressive." I said.

"What is?" asked the Indian guy who'd come to escort me to my new home.

"These motion sensors."

"Motion sensors?"

"The lights—they turned on when we walked in."

He chuckled. "Oh no, I just hit the switch when I opened the door. The lights are just slow to turn on."

I laughed, feeling a little silly, and then glanced at the stairs. "How do people carry heavy luggage up these stairs?"

"With the sheer desire to get to bed. By the time people lug their bags up here, they're usually so tired they just want to crash."

"Sounds about right. I'm exhausted, too. Didn't get much sleep on the flight."

He helped me haul my bags to the apartment. When we entered, I was taken aback by the space. A huge lounge area that could easily fit 20 people, no TV but a projector and screen, six dining tables, each with four chairs, and two shared computers for communal use. I noticed three doors at the end of a hallway.

"This place is massive for just six people. I might stay here forever."

"What are you talking about?" he asked.

"I mean, maybe not forever, but longer than I thought."

"No, I meant what about the six people?"

"The ad said six people in four rooms—two shared rooms, two individual rooms."

He smirked. "Did it actually say that?"

"Well, it said six people in four rooms, and I assumed the rest."

"Prepare to be surprised." he said as he walked past me, opening the door behind me. "This is your room."

I turned to see three bunk beds crammed into a tiny space. The door to my bed was just two steps away, and there was no way anyone could take more than three steps straight without hitting a bed. Six small wardrobes stood in the corner, each smaller than my suitcase.

"Surprised?" he asked, seeing my stunned expression.

"Uh, yeah."

"Six people in four rooms means six people in *each* of the four rooms. So, 24 people live here in total. And that's your bed." he said, pointing to a lower bunk.

I was too exhausted to think. I nodded, thanked him, and shoved my bags under the bed, too cold and tired to unpack. As I lay down, I realised my blanket was still in my suitcase. I started to pull it out when the door opened again.

"Hey, I'm Jack. I was asleep when you called. Sorry for not answering earlier." said a tall guy, holding out a heavy blanket.

"No problem, the other guy helped me get in."

"Here's your linen." he said, handing over the blanket that felt like it weighed more than me.

"Thanks. I really need to sleep now. I'm wiped out."

"Understandable. Catch you later, mate." Jack said, closing the door behind him.

I checked the time—9:15. Without bothering to change, I crawled into bed, pulled the blanket over me, and fell asleep almost instantly.

When I woke up, it took me a moment to remember where I was. For a split second, I imagined getting a fresh breakfast from my mum. I sat up, only to smack my head against the top bunk. The loud bang woke up the Chinese guy sleeping above me.

"Hey, I'm Frank." he said, rubbing his eyes.

"Hi, I'm Jaideep. Just got here this morning. When did you arrive?"

He said something, but I couldn't understand.

"Sorry, could you repeat that?"

He spoke again, but I still couldn't make sense of it. After a few more failed attempts, I realised neither of us understood the other. I started wondering if all the English I learned in India was wrong. Maybe I couldn't understand him, and he couldn't understand me.

Just as I was puzzling over how to communicate, I checked my watch. It was 4:30 and the sky was pitch dark. I'd slept for 20 hours straight—through an entire day. No missed calls, not even from Mum, which surprised me.

I heard loud cheering from the living room and wondered why people were so excited this early in the morning. I opened the door to find nearly 20 people watching a game with an oval ball, where bulky players collided like bumper cars.

"What game is this?" I asked someone walking past.

"It's Australian football." he replied.

"Why's it happening so early? Are they playing overseas?"

"No, it's at the MCG."

I understood then that it wasn't 4:30 a.m. but 4:30 p.m. It gets dark early in Melbourne. Homesickness hit me hard just then. I missed my mum, dad, brother, friends, cousins, uncles, aunts—everyone. I called home to let them know I'd arrived safely, and after hearing their voices, I felt a bit better.

I went back out and asked one of my roommates, "MCG stands for Melbourne Cricket Ground, right? Why are they playing some other game there?"

"What's cricket?" he asked.

I was stunned. How could someone not know about cricket in a country that had won five World Cups? He must be joking, but I kept the thought to myself.

As I walked back to my room, I knew my English was probably fine—after all, the locals understood me. Maybe Frank was in the same boat as me, struggling with a new environment. With a sigh of relief, I lay down on my bed again, finally feeling like things might just work out.

As I was watching something on my mobile, a guy walked into the room and placed his bag on the lower bunk to my left. Another roommate. I gave him a quick smile and went back to my YouTube video. He grabbed his towel and left the room, returning a little while later looking fresh after a shower.

I extended my hand. "Hi, I'm Jaideep. Just arrived today."

"Hey, I'm Krish. I've been living here for a while now." he said with a smile. "Nice to meet you. Where are you from?"

"Mumbai, India. And you?"

"People often mistake me for being Indian, but I'm from Sri Lanka."

"Nice! Sri Lanka is a beautiful country."

"Have you been there?" Krish asked.

"No, I've only seen it on TV during cricket matches. That's how I've seen most places in the world."

"Is that why you chose to come to Australia?" Krish sounded amused.

"Yeah." I chuckled.

"You'll be surprised to know that not many people actually follow cricket here."

"Yeah, I just met a guy in the living room who didn't even know what cricket was!"

Krish laughed. "Most of the people here are European. They don't really follow it."

"Oh." I replied, followed by a long pause. To keep the conversation going, I asked, "You look tired. Long day?"

"Yeah, just finished work. Saturdays are crazy because we have to inbound all the materials, remove expired items, and prepare for Sunday's restocking."

"Sounds busy. So, you work here? I thought this place was for students only."

"I am a student, at the University of Melbourne. But I work part-time to stay on top of my finances."

"Oh, nice! Is it hard to find a part-time job here?"

"It can be if you don't have any references, but if you do, it's pretty straightforward. Otherwise, you just have to keep trying."

Sensing he was open for more conversation, I asked, "Where do you work?"

"At the 7-Eleven around the corner." he said, gesturing towards the window.

I shrugged, not knowing where he meant.

"Don't worry, it's your first day. You'll see it when you leave. Pretty much everyone who lives here visits that 7-Eleven every day."

"Okay. What exactly is a 7-Eleven?"

"It's a convenience store where you can grab coffee and every-day essentials." he explained, noticing my confusion. "You'll get it when you see it, probably tomorrow."

"Yeah, I'll have to look for a part-time job myself." I said, seizing the opportunity.

"What kind of job are you thinking about?"

"Preferably an office job." I laughed, and Krish joined in. "But like everyone else, I'll probably start from the bottom."

"That's the spirit! Got any ideas?"

"A friend in the U.S. suggested working in restaurants. He said it's great because it covers food and pays well."

"Maybe in the U.S., but not here. In restaurants, you usually only work two hours during lunch and four hours for dinner. They close between those times, so you'd have to leave and come back. It's not as convenient."

"Ah, so there goes my plan." I said, shaking my head. "What would you recommend?"

"I'd say try a convenience store, like where I work. The shifts are longer, the pay is decent, and the work is manageable. Plus, you get time to study during your shift."

"That sounds good. But what about food?"

"Cooking isn't too hard. You'll mess up the first couple of times, but after that, you'll get the hang of it."

"All right, I'll give it a shot. I've learned a few basics. How do I go about getting a job at a convenience store?"

"Make a résumé and, to be honest, you'll need to add a bit of fake experience. Say you worked in a store back in India. Then, go in person to every store and hand in your résumé. Mention you've got experience with restocking, inventory and cashier duties. Most résumés get tossed out, but if they need someone, you'll get lucky. They don't even read most of it; they just check your contact info."

"Sounds simple enough."

"Yeah, applying is easy, but finding an opening is tough. Everyone's looking for a similar job. Keep your options open for barista gigs and restaurants, too. Also, make sure you visit the stores between six and nine in the morning."

"Why that early?"

"That's when the owners or managers are there, tallying the previous day's earnings."

"Got it. I'll start working on my résumé for stores and restaurants tomorrow."

"Let me know if you need any help." Krish said, making his bed. "I'm going to sleep now—got an early start tomorrow."

"Good night. And let me know if you hear about any jobs at your store."

"Will do. Goodnight."

My first night ended with a shiver that ran up from my feet, through my limbs and along my spine. My feet had slipped out from under the quilt and the cold hit me hard. The windows were fogged up with condensation, and I couldn't see anything outside. The weak sunlight barely made it through. I checked my phone—minus two degrees Celsius. I quickly pulled my feet back under the quilt, trying to get warm or, at the very least, stay alive.

After a while, hunger forced me out of the bed. Krish had already left for work, and his bed was neatly made.

"It's freezing." I muttered to the guy sleeping a few feet away.

"It's normal in Melbourne." he replied without opening his eyes. "It's always cold here."

"Oh." I said, forcing a grin. "Do you know where I can get some eggs or potatoes nearby?"

"Yeah, the Victoria Street Market, just down the street. You'll find fresh vegetables and eggs there."

"Thanks. Are there any utensils in the kitchen?"

"Yeah, but make sure you wash them immediately. Otherwise, you'll get fined fifty dollars."

"Fifty bucks? That's steep."

"People wouldn't keep it clean otherwise."

"Fair enough." I said, getting dressed. Jeans, a T-shirt, a sweater, a jacket, and a beanie. "Today's my first attempt at cooking. Let's hope it goes well."

I stepped outside into my dream country. The cold was sharp, but the air was fresh, and the quiet in the city centre felt surreal. There was no traffic—just peaceful streets lined with bike paths marked with green paint and white bicycle symbols.

At the first intersection, I stopped, looking for cars, but the streets were empty. Then, I noticed a small black panel with a circular steel push-button on a pole. I was trying to figure out what it was for, when a young Asian boy ran up and pressed it. Immediately, a strange sound came from the pole, signalling it was safe to cross. His parents caught up to him, glanced at me, and pulled him back, whispering, "He's sick, stay away."

I just smiled and walked away slowly, taking in the quiet streets. After a few blocks, I reached the Victoria Market and bought eggs, potatoes and bananas. I returned home, ready to cook.

In the kitchen, I tried to recall how to make an omelette. I chopped a quarter of an onion—thinking it was my first time doing that—then cracked an egg into a bowl and added a bit of salt. But it felt like too much salt, so I added another egg. Then, it seemed like too little salt, so I sprinkled a bit more, which felt like too much again. In a panic, I added one more egg and left it at that. I thought I'd nailed it.

Everything went fine until it was time to flip the omelette. As I turned it over, the other side was burnt black, letting out a horrible smell. I sighed, turned off the gas, and threw the whole thing away.

Now what? I was still hungry. Back home, food was always ready, and if it wasn't on the table, I could get some street food nearby. Then I spotted the potatoes and bananas.

I grabbed a banana to hold me over, then set my sights on the potatoes. I sliced them thin, heated oil in the pan, and threw them in. After stirring them a bit, I added salt, turmeric, and chili powder. Remembering my earlier mistake, I made sure not to leave them on the stove for too long. When they looked ready, I proudly plated them with some toast.

On my way to the dining table, I announced to my room-mates, "I cooked for the first time, and it smells amazing."

One of them smiled as I sat down to eat.

I took my first bite. The potatoes were raw. I had overcompensated, pulling them off the stove too soon. Frustrated, I grabbed two more bananas and gave up on cooking for the day.

I'd slept too much the previous night and couldn't nap. With nothing to do, I remembered that tomorrow was Monday, and I needed to go to the university for enrolment. I pulled up Google Maps and searched for the Royal Melbourne Institute of Technology. The first result said, "Melbourne Institute of Technology." Thinking that was it, I got dressed and headed out.

It was Sunday afternoon, and the city had a quiet, peaceful vibe. I passed by a 7-Eleven—so that's what Krish had mentioned.

I walked in, curious about what a convenience store looked like here. It was just a regular shop with a fancy name. After browsing for a bit, I continued walking, passing some closed shops.

I reached a long, historic three-storey building with giant doors and two massive columns flanking the steps. The architecture looked impressive, but I couldn't tell what it was. I figured I had two years to find that out and kept walking. A few steps later, I noticed a massive banner on the building that said, "Tony Abbott is an asshole." I thought it was a movie promotion and moved on.

I kept following Google Maps, eventually reaching what it said was my destination. But to my dismay, I couldn't find the iconic RMIT building I had seen all over the internet. Instead, I found a yellow building with "Melbourne University of Technology" written on it in blue. I had been fooled.

Disoriented and disappointed, I took a deep breath and told myself, "Everything will be fine. Relax. Don't panic. Don't tell anyone yet. Let's wait for orientation tomorrow and figure things out."

I turned on Google Maps again to find my way back home and decided to call my friends in India to share my misery.

As I walked up La Trobe Street, first I reached the intersection of Swanston Street and spotted a giant library to my right. It looked impressive. I turned left as Google Maps directed. And there it was: Royal Melbourne Institute of Technology. I couldn't believe my eyes. This multi-storey building, with its distinctive and eclectic architectural style, appeared to be part of an urban setting with several people and vehicles in the foreground.

The lower part of the building featured classic architecture with red brick walls and white stone trim. Its windows were large and multi-paned, typical of early 20th-century commercial architecture. The roof and upper part of the building had a modern, artistic design element, featuring large, irregularly shaped, green structures that resembled organic forms or abstract sculptures, creating a striking contrast with the more traditional architecture below.

Pedestrians, including a group of people walking on the pavement, and a few vehicles, including a silver car and white vans, indicated an active urban environment. Then I saw street signs, traffic lights and a black sign with white text reading "INFO." the information centre of my university. Now I knew where I'd have to come tomorrow morning.

I closed eyes, pocketed my mobile and with a smile started walking ahead with the gaze towards the building. I kept walking straight on Swanston Street and passed a KFC. I was looking for the building I saw on the internet. I crossed the road and went on the other side of the road to see a strikingly modern architectural structure over the KFC. The building featured a highly irregular shape with curves and undulations vastly different from the conventional straight lines and right angles typical of traditional architecture. The facade's triangular panels weren't uniform in size or orientation, contributing to the building's organic and fluid appearance.

The colour palette of this building was bold and varied, making it stand out. Its grey panels provided a neutral base; yellow and orange panels added warmth and vibrancy; its black panels created contrast and depth.

The entrance to the building is a large, red structure that contrasts sharply with the surrounding panels. On a panel were the logo and name of the building, "RMIT".

After a bit more exploring, I headed back home, feeling I'd accomplished enough for the first day. I called Amar.

"Hello, what are you doing?"

"I just saw the university, and it looks even better than it did on the computer screen."

"Nice! You're enjoying it there, right?"

"Yeah, I am." Lying felt like the easiest thing to do at the time. I knew I'd left my parents and brother far behind. I was out of my comfort zone, homesick and struggling with food. I hadn't eaten much, except for a few bananas, and there wasn't much hope for anything else. But at least I was at peace, if not happy. I knew it would be hard for them to understand. I had my dreams; they had taught me to dream. They'd given me the confidence to leave home, to not be afraid of challenges, and to face them head-on. So, I'd keep saying I was happy from now on. "I hope you are all doing well, too."

"Yes, we're fine. But Mum and Dad are a little worried about you. Other than that, everything's good."

"That's good. What time is it there now?"

"Five-thirty."

"Still early. What are your plans for the evening?"

"Probably watch something on the laptop. I just got a new Acer."

"Nice. What specs does it have?"

"Nothing special, just a basic one to start with. I'll upgrade later if I need to."

"Fair enough. What else are you up to?"

"Thinking of watching *Friends* or *The Big Bang Theory* on the laptop."

"Good choices. What do you have on your hard drive?"

"Just Microsoft Office and a couple of Bollywood movies— *Andaz Apna Apna* and *Hera Pheri*."

"Why Microsoft Office?"

"It's expensive to buy here, so I bought it on the hard drive. I'll install it later."

"Smart move."

"That's me." I chuckled.

He laughed, then asked, "What's for dinner?"

"I had a big lunch, so I'm just going to make some Maggi later."

"Sounds good. I've got to hit the books now. Talk later?"

"All right, study hard."

"Will do." He hung up.

After the call, I reflected on the day with a sense of quiet satisfaction. I powered up my new laptop, connected the hard drive and started watching *Friends*. After a few episodes and a quick bowl of Maggi, I decided to call it a night. Tomorrow was another day to look forward to.

Next morning, I woke wrapped in a blanket like an awkward, unwanted gift. Sunlight filtered through the room's only window. Today was the day to make new friends. Hopefully, I'd be able to communicate in English—or better yet, maybe I'd find someone who spoke Hindi. With that hope, I pulled off the blanket, dragged myself out of bed, placed my feet on the cold floor, and got ready to leave within 20 minutes. Stepping outside, I looked up at the sky and began my walk to the building I had seen the night before, showing the sign "INFO".

The city buzzed with people heading to work. It was Monday, and everyone seemed fresh, ready to start their week with a burst of energy. There was a spring in their step, and I fed off that energy, putting one foot in front of the other until I reached my destination.

A queue had already formed for enrolment, so I joined it and pulled out my documents, ready for my turn. An Indian guy stood in front of me. I glanced at his form—his name was Vikram Mane. To my delight, not only was he from India, but he was from the same state as me. I waited for him to turn around so I could start a conversation. And then, as if on cue, he did.

"Hi, Jaideep." I said, extending my hand.

"Hi, Vikram." he replied, shaking it.

"Where are you from?" I went straight to the point.

"Nagpur. You?"

"Mumbai."

"Nice. When did you get here?"

"Two days ago. What about you?"

"I've been here about 20 days now. Came early for the induction."

"My visa was delayed. I only got it 12 days ago, so I missed the induction."

"Eh, you didn't miss much. It was mostly useless." Vikram said with a shrug. "Where are you staying?"

"277 Queensberry Street, just a few minutes from here. It's a four-bedroom place, but 24 people are staying there." I paused, waiting for his reaction. He raised his eyebrows but didn't say anything. "Where do you stay?"

"Tarneit, about an hour from here."

"Why stay so far? There are plenty of places in the city. I found several when I was looking."

"My cousin lives in Tarneit, so I'm staying with him for now. Once classes start and I make more friends, I'll look for a place closer. Is your accommodation tied to any fixed period?"

"No, I can cancel with two weeks' notice."

"Great. I met a couple of guys from Kolhapur and Bhopal during induction. They're also looking for roommates. Maybe the four of us can search for a place together."

"That works for me. Let's meet them and start looking." I nodded for him to look ahead as it was his turn to submit his documents.

The staff took his papers, verified them and asked him to step in front of the camera. They clicked his photo, and within minutes, he had his ID card. Soon, I received mine as well.

I saw Vikram chatting with another Indian guy who sounded South Indian and spoke fluent English. Feeling hesitant to join in, I walked over and stood next to Vikram as they talked.

"Hi, I'm Rohan." the guy said, extending his hand towards me.

"Hey, Jaideep. Are you also looking for a place to stay?"

"No, he's loaded." Vikram cut in with a grin. "He's living in RMIT Village, right around the corner. Costs a fortune per week."

"It's not that bad." Rohan said.

"So, what's the plan now? When do your classes start?" I asked. "Mine start tonight at 6 p.m. Such a weird time—six to nine, every evening from Monday to Thursday. Why would they do that?"

"A lot of people here are part-time students." Rohan explained. "They work during the day, so most of the master's classes are in the evening."

"Ah, makes sense." I nodded. "Hey, do you know where the MCG is? Google Maps says it's nearby."

"Yeah, you can see it from Flinders Street Station. I pass by it every time I come to campus." Vikram chimed in.

"Let's walk there and talk on the way." Rohan suggested, and we agreed.

As we walked, we exchanged details about our qualifications and work experience. Eventually, the conversation shifted to why we had chosen Australia. They were surprised when I told them I only ever wanted to come to Australia, unlike many others who considered it a second choice. Listening to their stories, I became conscious they were quite well off. I'd need to find friends who were more in my league.

Later, the topic turned to the challenges we'd faced since arriving.

"I've only been here two days." I said. "The only real challenges so far are the cold weather and food. I've mostly been eating Maggi and bananas."

Rohan pointed to a nearby sign. "See that 'Om Vegetarian'? You can get unlimited Indian food there for six dollars. It's pretty decent for the price."

He was a godsend. This would solve my food problem for the time being. I thanked him silently, tipping my head slightly as if thanking the heavens, too.

In my mind, I was already calculating the route to get there on my own—taking the tram seemed the most practical option. Just as I finished figuring it out, I noticed a vintage building ahead, with people streaming in and out. "What's that building?" I asked.

"That's Flinders Street Station." Vikram replied.

We kept walking and soon we crossed an intersection. I was admiring the station to my right when Vikram pointed left. "And that's Federation Square."

"Where's the MCG?" I asked.

We walked across a bridge, and just as I was still taking in the station's architecture, Vikram said, "There it is—the MCG."

I turned my gaze from the station and looked left. A calm river stretched below us, with barely a ripple. It reflected the trees and sky above. On either side of the river, lush green trees lined the banks and a small park with neatly trimmed grass and pathways sat to the right. The river flowed straight ahead before bending to the right.

Just beyond the bend, the stadium appeared—the MCG, a place I'd seen countless times on TV. Its familiar roof and towering light structures loomed in the distance, standing tall. As I stared at it, a wave of nostalgia hit me, and I began to replay all the matches I'd watched over the years, imagining the roaring crowds and the iconic games that had unfolded on that ground.

"I had the chance to watch the India vs. South Africa game during the last World Cup." I said, still gazing at the serene sight of the MCG. "But I didn't go."

"How'd that happen?" Rohan asked.

"Well, I used to work at Bajaj Electricals. They had this program where any dealer doing more than one crore worth of business would be sponsored by Bajaj to attend the match. A few company employees went along, too."

"So why didn't you go?" Rohan asked, eyebrows raised. "That game was incredible."

"If I'd known it'd be that good, I definitely would've gone." I replied, pausing for a while before adding, "But honestly, the invite caught me off guard. I thought they were messing with me. Besides, I knew I was coming to Melbourne in a few months anyway. I figured if I didn't like this place, it would put a dampner on my plans from the start."

"It's a good place to be." Vikram said.

"I know that now." I said with a grin. "From now on, I'm not missing any big games here."

I was lost in thought when Rohan nudged me. "Time for my lecture. Let's head back."

"All right." I nodded, following him.

Rohan's lecture started at 4 p.m., and Vikram and I had two hours to kill before ours. As we reached the university, we saw a bunch of food stalls—sponsored by the university, no less. To my delight, I stuffed myself before we began strolling around.

Walking from one building to another, we had to dodge city traffic—cars, trams, buses, even bicycles on the footpath. It made me wonder aloud, "Is this university in the city, or is the city inside the university?"

Vikram chuckled, nodding. "And where does it end? The map says our Engineering Department is in Building 86. It's at the far end of RMIT. I hope there's a tram stop there."

"Which street is it on?"

"Queensberry Street."

"Oh, I live on Queensberry Street." I said before quickly correcting myself, "Well, I live *in* a house on Queensberry Street. And there's a tram stop nearby."

As we continued walking, we passed a building with what looked like a huge movie poster saying "Tony Abbot Is an Asshole" plastered on it. I pointed to it. "Have you seen that movie?"

Vikram grinned. "That's not a movie. That's the Prime Minister of Australia."

"What? Seriously?"

"Yep."

"This is freedom of speech on another level."

Vikram grinned. "Australia's pretty free, man. We'll figure it out as we go."

Puffing, we eventually reached Building 86. Down the road, a few blocks away, we spotted a tram stop. We swapped glances, climbed the stairs and started searching for our classrooms. After exchanging numbers, we split up. Vikram found his room, already full of students chatting and networking. He waved me off, promising to call after the lecture.

I continued my search, eventually finding my room—completely empty. I approached a staff member nearby and asked if I had the right place. He nodded, though I wasn't sure if he actually understood me or just preferred sign language.

Looking around at the empty classroom, I grasped what the agency meant when they said there were no Indians in my branch—there was *nobody* in my batch. The classroom had ten rows of seats, so I had my pick. Backbenchers are for the settled, first bench is for the nerds. Since I was paying so much for this degree, I figured I might as well lean towards the nerds, so settled in the second row.

I had about 30 minutes to kill before the lecture started, so I pulled out my laptop, connected to the university wi-fi, and browsed the internet. With around 14 minutes left, six Asian students walked in. I felt a wave of relief—at least I wasn't alone. They headed straight to the back row. Smart kids, I figured. They probably already know everything.

Three minutes later, five Australians strolled in, all of them looking like they were over 45. "Isn't it a bit late to do a master's, mate?" I muttered to myself in a terrible Aussie accent.

It was settled—I wasn't making any new friends today. But just four minutes before class, an Indian guy walked in, lost in his own world. I stared at him, mentally shouting, "COME SIT NEXT TO ME!"

As if he heard me, he looked my way and walked over, extending his hand. "Govind."

"Jaideep." I said, shaking his hand.

"Where are you from?" he asked, settling in.

"Mumbai."

"I was in Mumbai till the eighth grade, in Sion. Then my dad got transferred to Kerala, and we moved."

"Oh, cool. I'm from Panvel—not really *Mumbai* Mumbai, but close enough. Thank God you showed up. I thought there weren't any Indians in this branch. My counsellor even warned me about it."

"Don't worry." he chuckled. "There are a few. Two from Kerala, two from Maharashtra, one from Gujarat, and one from Rajasthan."

"Nice! At least there are people I can talk to."

Just then, a group of Indian students speaking Malayalam walked in and greeted Govind. They introduced themselves: Sagar, Mahesh, Rounak, Kunal, Sarthak and Gaurav. We had a good chat for the next few minutes as the classroom filled up. I was surprised to see almost 40 Asians, ten Indians, and only five Australians. I expected more locals, but it seemed this course wasn't their preference.

The professor entered, and the class quieted down.

After the lecture, we all had a chat about accommodation and settling in. A bonding session was planned for the weekend. Everyone lived nearby, but I still felt a bit left out since most of them knew each other before arriving in Melbourne. I was the lone stranger.

Sometimes, though, being alone has its perks. Next morning I caught up with Vikram, Madhur and Rounak, who were also looking for a place to stay, and needed a fourth person for shared accommodation. They invited me to join, but I told them I'd already paid a month's rent elsewhere. Jokingly, I added that I wouldn't pay rent until my current lease was up. They took it seriously and agreed I didn't need to pay for the first few days.

"I don't have a bank account yet." I told the group.

"There's a Commonwealth Bank on campus." Rounak suggested. "It's easier to open an account there, compared to other banks. They only need your Confirmation of Enrolment (COE) from the university, unlike other banks that require proof of address and more documents. I'm heading that way, so I'll show you where it is."

"Thanks." I said, and we walked together. We chatted about random things, admiring the city's beauty and its people. Before long, we arrived at the bank. Rounak pointed me towards an attendant and said, "Just go to them, and they'll sort you out." He waved goodbye. "See you later."

I approached the attendant. "Hi, I need to open a bank account. I just arrived in Melbourne last week. How do I go about it?"

"We can definitely help with that. Head to that office, and someone will assist you shortly."

A few minutes later, a woman greeted me. She was so striking that I barely heard what she said after her initial hello. She must've noticed because she repeated, "Why did you choose Comm Bank?"

Snapping out of it, I smiled. "Last year, India played a cricket series sponsored by Commonwealth Bank. India won, and I decided right then that I'd open an account with Comm Bank when I get here. I guess fate brought me here today."

She looked surprised. "Good to know those sponsorships pay off like that."

"I don't know about others, but I'm definitely here because of that—and because India won. If they'd lost, maybe I'd be at a different bank right now."

She laughed. "Well, we're glad to have you. Let's get your account set up." After taking my passport and COE, she entered the information on her computer while I tried not to stare. "All done. You'll get an email confirmation, and your debit card will arrive at your address in two business days."

"Thanks." I said, and I left.

A few days later, after settling into uni and making friends, Madhur called me.

"One of our seniors is subletting his place in the city. It's central and will be convenient for commuting. Vikram and Rounak aren't around, so I was wondering if you'd like to come with me to check it out."

I felt a small sense of pride. Someone needed me! "Sure. What time?" I asked, trying not to sound too eager.

"In about half an hour?"

"Okay, send me the address. I'll see you there."

It was only a ten-minute walk. When I arrived, Madhur was already there, glued to his phone like everyone else waiting for something.

"How'd you find this place?" I asked.

He hadn't seen me arrive. He startled then smiled. "Our seniors are subletting it. I found them on Gumtree. They graduated this year and need a bigger place because their parents are coming to visit."

"Why didn't they just get a shorter lease to begin with?"

"Who knows? Why does it matter to you?" He grinned, and I dropped the topic.

We started chatting about uni when a guy came out and greeted Madhur. We followed him to see the apartment. The building had a mean-looking blonde receptionist, and our guide advised us to avoid talking to her, no matter what. We got into the elevator, and he pressed the button for the 20th floor.

"Nice." I thought. "20th floor, this should be fun."

The elevator ride felt like an eternity, and I couldn't tell if it was slow or if 20 floors were just that high. But finally, we arrived. The corridor was bright and carpeted—looking good so far.

The guy opened the apartment door. Grey carpet through-out. To the right was the kitchen and a bathroom. Straight ahead, a huge living area with two adjacent bedrooms on the right. But the real highlight was the balcony view.

Across the road, a corporate building stood tall. I could see people in suits, working hard. One day, that'll be me, I thought. The panoramic view stretched from Etihad Stadium on the left to Parliament Station on the right.

I was sold. I wanted to live here. But I had to be cautious—my finances weren't looking great. They'd already agreed to waive my first rent payment, so I needed to be respectful of the others' opinions.

As I enjoyed the view, I overheard Madhur talking about the apartment's availability. The tenant confirmed it was available this week if we were interested. Madhur asked them not to show it to anyone else until tomorrow, when our other two prospective roommates could see it. "We'll all be here tomorrow at the same time." Madhur confirmed.

"Thanks for checking!" I thought, but smiled politely.

Next day, we all met at the apartment again. I was late, try-ing not to seem too eager. "Hi, everyone." I greeted, shaking hands.

"This place is great—everything's nearby." Rounak said excit-edly, pointing in all directions. "QVB (Queen Victoria Building), RMIT, the station, tram stops ..."

"Let's go in." said another guy, stepping out of the door.

"That's his roommate." Madhur whispered.

We went through the same routine, except this time, the mean blonde receptionist was loudly arguing with someone.

"This is a good spot." Vikram remarked.

"Wait until you see the balcony." I said.

In no time, we were discussing moving dates. The tenants wanted out as soon as possible, and Vikram suggested we move in next week. Everyone agreed—no one even checked with me, though I couldn't move in for three more weeks.

We wrapped up the visit by heading to the concierge to change the tenancy. The paperwork was sorted quickly, and the keys were ours within a couple of days.

After collecting the keys, Vikram moved in first. I helped him with his luggage, and Rounak and Madhur followed suit. Slowly, I moved in, too.

I had friends, I'd started my master's and settled into life here. But I'd lost track of financial planning. I'd spent half my savings on rent and deposit, and the rest on food, winter clothes, clubbing, and even a visit to a strip club with new friends. Checking my bank app, I saw I was out of money.

It had been years since I asked my dad for money. But now, I had no choice.

"Hello, Papa, how are you?"

"What do you need?" he replied, sensing the purpose of my call.

"I need money. I spent most of what I brought on rent and deposit, and eating out every day."

"You said you'd look for a part-time job. What happened to that plan?"

"I'm looking. My friend and I are going to apply together."

"Why haven't you started already?"

"I'm waiting for him to join me. I'm nervous about job-hunting alone."

"Since when?"

"About a week now."

"And any leads?"

"Not yet. We haven't really started because he's still jet-lagged."

"How is he managing his expenses?"

"His aunt in the U.S. is sending him money for now."

"Do you think he's in a rush to look for a job if he's getting help?"

"He says he is."

"And what about you? What's holding you back?"

"It's just cold, Papa. Hard to wake up early."

"Since when have you had trouble waking up early?"

"It's not me, it's my friend."

"Listen, you don't have anyone in the U.S. sending you money. It's just me. Whatever you spend, your brother will go without. So, you will need to start earning yourself now."

That hit hard. I hadn't considered how my actions were affecting my brother.

"I'll send you $4,000, but that's the last time. After that, if you need more, I'll send you a plane ticket back home."

"But I've only been here 22 days ..."

"You can stay as long as you want, but you'll need to fund it yourself. Got it?"

"Okay."

"And don't wait for others. Do it yourself."

"Yes, Papa."

Hanging up, I thought, the pressure was real, now. I had to find a job. Remembering a conversation with Krish, I headed to the library, drafted resumes for every type of job—convenience stores, barista roles, supermarkets, cleaning, even car washes. After spending a couple of hours on it, I printed ten copies of each. With the day's lecture done, I grabbed a bite and went home.

Madhur noticed my mood. "What's up? You seem down."

"I spoke to my dad today. He will cut me off. I either find a job, or I'm heading back."

"Your dad's tough."

"Yeah. Can't change that now."

NOTHING GOOD COMES EASILY

Waking up at 5 a.m., I was hit by the freezing cold. Even breathing felt like a chore. But I knew I had to push through; the potential payoff was huge. I got dressed, ready for whatever that lay ahead. The process was clear in my mind—I knew what I had to do, the usual outcomes, and the best-case scenario. I just had to stay confident and get it done.

I left home around 5:45 a.m., determined to be at each store as they opened, when the managers or owners were around. My first stop was Ezymart at Melbourne Central Station. *It's a busy station; they probably need more help* I thought. I pulled out my resume, detailing my experience working in a store in India, and walked in.

Being naturally shy, I waited until the store was less crowded before approaching the counter. "Hi, how are you?" I asked nervously.

"Very good, how are you?" the clerk replied.

"I'm good, too. I was wondering if you're hiring? I'm looking for a part-time job."

"Not right now, but you can leave your resume. If something comes up, we'll call you."

"Thanks." I said, handing over my resume and stepping out. One down.

Next was a 7-Eleven. The process was the same, but this time when I asked, "Are you hiring?" the clerk barely glanced at me and called out, "Next." to the person behind me.

"Can you at least keep my resume?" I asked, passing it to him.

"Sure." he muttered, snatching the paper. As I turned to leave, I saw his reflection, crumpling it and tossing it into the trash.

Two attempts in, and I'd already seen the best and worst reactions. On to the next.

I approached a small café where a girl was making morning coffees. "Hi." I said. "Looks like your coffee is popular. Must be a busy place."

"Yeah, mornings are hectic, especially from seven to nine. It calms down after that, then picks up again after lunch."

"Do you handle all this on your own?"

"I do. If it gets too crazy, I call the owners—they live nearby and can help out in a few minutes."

"That's great! I'm actually looking for a job, and I'm really interested in working here."

"Have you made coffee before?" she asked, giving me a doubtful look.

"Not exactly, but I've taken orders and worked around coffee in India. I'd love to help, even if it's just taking orders."

"I don't make the hiring decisions." she said. "You'll have to talk to the owners."

"When are they usually here? I can come back."

"They don't have a set time. They show up if I need help. You'll just have to try your luck."

"How about you call them now and tell them it's busy? I'll help out, and when they arrive, I'll be here!"

She raised an eyebrow. "No. I'm not doing that."

"Okay, can you at least keep my resume?"

"Sure." She took it, and I left, feeling slightly deflated but happy I'd actually had a decent conversation with her.

After that, I decided to try the big grocery chains. I headed to Woolworths and asked, "Is the store manager in today?"

"Yes." said the attendant. "I'll call him for you."

A tall, serious-looking man came out. "Hi, I hear you wanted to see me? Any issues with the store?"

"No, no problems. I'm a student at RMIT and just wanted to know if you have any vacancies."

"You'll need to check online, mate. All our hiring is centralised now."

"I was told managers used to hire directly?"

"That was a while back. Everything's online these days. Same goes for Coles."

"Okay, thanks. I guess I'll try Aldi next."

He laughed lightly. "They're all the same, mate. Apply online. But hey, good luck!"

By then, I'd had enough rejections for one day. I headed home by 10 a.m. Vikram was awake, waiting for an update. "How did it go?"

"Lots of rejections. I hit two stores, one café, and Woolworths. Only four places."

"That's it? You said you needed a job by the end of the week, and you only went to four places?"

I shrugged. "It's a start. At least I learned something."

"What's that?"

"That this won't be easy." I said with a laugh, and he joined in.

"By the way, I made chicken curry this morning. Help yourself." he said.

I took a bite. "Wow, this is amazing! How'd you make it?"

"My mum runs a catering business. I called her and followed her instructions."

"Well, you nailed it." I said, feeling full and content for the first time in days. After the meal, I slipped into a food coma, finally able to forget the stress for a while. I needed a nap before my evening lecture anyway.

As I drifted off, I felt the weight of my situation lift, if only temporarily. In my dreams, everything was perfect—my wishes fulfilled, my heart content. I always found it ironic how I see dreams when I am asleep and in all my dreams, I am awake and full of life.

The next day followed the same routine. I got ready and left the house as quickly as possible. I hit the streets when the managers were still fresh, full of energy, and not yet worn down by the usual grind. I wandered around the streets of Melbourne CBD for a few hours, tired, frustrated and drained by the end of it, returning home without any success.

When I opened the door, Madhur was awake, sitting with Vikram.

"How was your day?" Madhur asked.

Vikram cut in, "Look at his face—he's tense. Nothing good happened today, huh?"

I nodded silently, heading straight for the couch, sinking into it as I stared up at the white ceiling of our apartment.

After a few minutes of space, Madhur came over. "Tell us what happened. You'll feel better. Everyone has ups and downs, and we haven't even started looking for jobs yet. When we do, we could use your experiences."

I sighed. "At 7-Eleven. The guy didn't even look at my resume—just tossed it onto a stack."

"How do you know it was a stack of resumes?" Madhur asked.

"Because he said, 'I'll add it to the resumes here.' Then I went to 17 other stores. No luck at any of them."

Madhur raised an eyebrow. "How do you know it was 17?"

"Because I brought 20 resumes. Went to two stores yesterday, and today, I finished the rest." I paused. "After that, I hit the cafes and restaurants. The restaurants weren't open yet, but I was already worn out from the cafes. Nineteen cafes, and nothing. At least yesterday, a cute girl spoke to me. Today? Not even that."

Vikram said, "Have you tried the IGA grocery store in our building?"

"First place I went." I replied, shaking my head.

"What about that convenience store across the street? City Convenience Store?"

"We pass that place every day. Ever see anyone inside?" I asked, watching Madhur nod. "Exactly. They don't need help if they don't have customers."

They both agreed.

"So, what now?" Vikram asked.

"I'm burning through my money fast. I need a job, and soon. I printed out 30 resumes for store jobs, 20 for car wash jobs, 20 more for cafes. Next, I'm applying for online jobs." I applied for online jobs at Woolworths and Coles and, within minutes, I received an email from Coles that my application has been denied. Then I go to Vikram and say, "There's something I'm not doing right. I need to change my approach, maybe try the suburbs. There might be some opportunity there."

"You'd need a car for that." Vikram said. "It's hard to get around the suburbs without one. Most places aren't close to train stations."

I sighed. "City it is, then." We all shared a knowing smile.

Madhur perked up. "You know, Chadstone Shopping Centre isn't too far. I want to pick up some stuff. You could come along and look for jobs there."

"Sounds like a plan. Where's Chadstone?"

"Uh ... Chadstone?"

I rolled my eyes. "Right, that makes sense. Let's go tomorrow. We'll leave early."

"No point." Madhur said. "The mall opens at ten."

"All right, we'll leave at nine and get there when it opens."

The rest of the day was calm. I applied for more random jobs online and immediately received rejection emails. But at least people were looking at my profile. Maybe someday someone would give me a chance.

The next morning, we woke up late, got ready, and reached Chadstone by ten. "See ya." I said to Madhur as we split at the entrance. "Call me when you're done."

"I'll wait in the food court." he replied, and we gave each other a thumbs-up.

I walked around, getting used to the environment, psyching myself up to walk into the next store I saw. Lovisa was the first one.

"Good morning! Looking for something for your girlfriend or mum?" the sales assistant chirped.

"Actually, both of them want me to get a job here. Do you have any vacancy?" I said, then saw this was a jewellery store.

She laughed. "Unfortunately, we only hire women here."

"Isn't that, uh, gender discrimination?"

"Yes, it is." she said with a grin. "And we take pride in it. Jokes aside, we don't have any openings right now. You can leave your resume, though, and we'll call if anything comes up."

"Thanks. That's all I can ask for."

"By the way, where do your girlfriend and mum live?"

"Mum's in India. The girlfriend? She only exists in my dreams."

She smiled. "Nice to know our store is famous beyond borders and reality."

I left Lovisa with a grin. Chatting with strangers was fun, but I needed money. A couple of hours later, Madhur texted me. "Where are you? I'm at the food court."

"On my way." I replied. "I'm out of resumes anyway."

When I got to the food court, Madhur was already eating. I felt a bit guilty dumping my problems on him, but I needed to vent. "I started with a jewellery store ..."

"Why jewellery?" he interrupted.

"Beggars can't be choosers." I shot back. "I went to Lovisa, some furniture shops, Strandbags, Petbarn, and a bunch of clothing stores. No luck anywhere. I even hit up the bookshops like Dymocks and kids' stores. Then Adidas, Nike and New Balance. No one has a job for me. I must be doing something wrong."

Madhur just sighed. "Eat something."

"What's the most efficient, economical food here?"

"Subway's decent. Get a chicken schnitzel."

"I've always hated Subway, but today might be the day."

"Why?"

"They ask too many questions. If I'm going to answer all that, I might as well make the sandwich myself. Why pay for it?"

I reluctantly went to Subway, answered a barrage of questions, and finally got to the counter. The attendant smiled. "Anything else?"

"Yeah, a job. Got any vacancies?"

He chuckled. "No, sorry. That'll be nine dollars."

"I'm not joking." I said, handing over my card. He nodded silently, and I left with my sandwich.

A week went by in a blur. I talked to everyone I met about finding a job, visiting every shop, café, restaurant, car wash, and even walking into open office doors. Soon, I began counting down the days based on the dwindling dollars in my account. It was terrifying—knowing I might not fulfil the dream that brought me here.

Worse, I wasn't proud of my efforts. It felt like I was failing myself. By Friday, I was drained—mentally and financially. I had just enough left to cover next month's rent. I didn't even know enough people here to ask for help; all my contacts were new. It wasn't the kind of bond where you could ask to borrow money, especially with no promise of when, or if, you could pay it back.

That day, I retraced my steps to the same stores I had visited the week before, pleading for part-time work or a reference—anything that might help me earn something. Another day, another string of rejections. I ended up at the Indian place Rohan had introduced me to a month earlier, where I'd been having combined late lunches and early dinners every day since Rohan introduced me to it, except when Vikram cooked.

I was weighed down with emotion as I headed to my evening lecture, telling myself that at least I'd learn something before I was forced to leave Australia for good. A small part of me tried to stay positive—at least I was trying with what little I had. I even thanked my parents in my head for giving me this chance to chase my dream, despite feeling like I'd let them down. Their hard-earned money was disappearing fast, and I had nothing to show for it. The thought that everyone in my family was struggling while I was wasting resources hit me hard. Now, I was part of the struggle, too.

During the lecture, my mind kept drifting. After class, I walked back to my place, exhausted and unsure of what my future held. I felt weak, and needed something to recharge. The nearest place to grab a Gatorade was the small City Convenience Store across from my building—the one I hadn't seen anyone inside for more than a month. I walked in, grabbed a bottle, and placed it on the counter.

"Hello." I said.

"Hey, how's it going?" the attendant asked, scanning the bottle. "Two ninety-five."

As I tapped it on the reader, he glanced at me and asked, "You look tired, bro. Everything all right?"

"I'm looking for a job. I've tried everywhere, but there's nothing out there." I said, feeling the weight of my words.

"What kind of job you looking for, mate?"

"Anything, really. I just need to make some money."

"Would you be up for working Friday, Saturday, and Sunday nights?"

"Absolutely." I said, the idea sparking some hope. "But I'm a student, so I can only work forty hours a fortnight."

"That's no problem." He scribbled something on a piece of paper and handed it to me. "Call this number on Monday. It's my uncle's. He's looking for someone to work here on weekend nights, but he can't find anyone, so I've been stuck here during prime time."

"Thank you, man. I'll call first thing Monday."

"Not too early." he chuckled. "We're Lebanese—trust me, we like to party, we live day life slow. Call around noon. He'll be up by then."

"Will do." I said, tucking the paper into my wallet. "Thanks again."

"No, thank you."

It was the first time I'd felt a real win since arriving. All the so-called "win-win" situations I'd been in were just business talk. This felt different. Walking out of the store, I felt a surge of energy, like the Gatorade was unnecessary. If I got this job, I'd finally catch a break. It was close to home and school. I could probably earn around a thousand dollars a month—enough to cover rent and still have a bit left for expenses. Things were starting to look up.

I spent the weekend thinking about it, keeping it to myself to avoid jinxing anything. Monday arrived, and I woke up with nervous anticipation. I spent the morning watching the clock, waiting for it to hit noon. By 11:45, I was out the door.

At 12 on the dot, I dialled the number. It rang three times before a deep voice answered, "Hello."

"Hi, I got your number from the guy working at City Convenience Store on Friday night. He mentioned you were looking for someone to work weekend nights."

"That's right."

"I'm looking for part-time work. Is the position still available?"

"Do you know where Crown is?"

"Yes." I replied, pulling up Google Maps. "It says it's an 18-minute walk. I can be there in about 15."

"Good. Call me when you get here, and I'll tell you where to meet."

"Thanks. See you soon."

I sprinted towards Crown, my heart racing, not just from the pace, but from the hope that this might be my break. I made it in 13 minutes, slightly out of breath, and called him. He gave me precise directions, clearly familiar with every corner of the place. Eventually, I spotted a man on the phone. "I see you." I said, hoping my guess was right.

He turned, meeting my gaze, and we walked towards each other. We shook hands, and as I caught my breath, he jumped right in. "How are you? How long have you been in Australia?"

"Thirty days now."

"Good. Where are you from?"

"India."

"Nice place." he said, nodding. "You're a student here?"

"Yes, I'm doing a master's in engineering management at RMIT City Campus."

"Where are you staying?"

"Lonsdale Street, just opposite the store."

He gave a small nod. "Ever worked as a cashier before?"

"Yes, I have." I lie. "Back in India. I worked as a cashier, handled inventory, restocked shelves, cleaned the store—whatever was needed." I could tell he sensed the exaggeration, but I held my ground.

"That's good. Any issue with selling cigarettes? Do you know the brands?"

"Yeah, I do—Marlboro, Benson & Hedges, Dunhill, Bond Street. I smoke, too." I pulled out my pack.

He smiled again, as if amused by my answers. "All right." he said. "Go to the same store now and start training. You'll meet Moe there. He'll train you, and based on his feedback, we'll decide what happens next."

"Thank you." I said, wondering whether to ask about the pay now or later.

He seemed to read my mind. "I'll pay you 15 dollars an hour for ten-hour shifts. Is that workable?"

"Yes, absolutely. But as a student, I can only work 40 hours a fortnight. Is that okay with you?"

"No problem. We'll manage."

Relief washed over me as I headed back to the store. The walk took about 20 minutes, because this time, I wasn't rushing. I soaked in the city's little details, enjoying the moment. For the first time, I was walking without the weight of uncertainty, with a smile on my face. I had a long way to go, but at least I had a lead.

Small victories started to feel significant, and I reminded myself to appreciate them. I thought about calling Dad, but decided to wait until everything was final.

When I arrived at the store, I approached the tall guy at the counter. "Hi, Moe? Sam told me to see you."

"Yeah, you must be Jaideep. Sam called about 15 minutes ago. You're early."

"Yeah, I really need this job ... well, actually, I need the money."

He chuckled. "And we need someone to work weekends. Come on in." He gestured for me to walk behind the counter.

As I stepped through, I noticed the cigarette stock beneath the counter, more valuable than anything else in the store. It had to be guarded with care.

"When did you arrive in Australia?" Moe asked.

"Almost a month ago. I'm studying at RMIT."

"Smart guy." he said with a smile.

I smiled back. "So, what do I need to do here?"

"It's pretty straightforward. When a customer walks in, greet them. Let them browse, then scan their items at the register. The price will show on both screens—one for us, one for them. Tell them the total, and if they pay in cash, enter the amount here, take the cash, and give them the change. If they pay by card, use this EFTPOS machine. Once the payment processes, put the first receipt in the till and ask if they need another copy. If they say no, hit 'No' on the machine. If they want it, hit 'Yes' and hand it over. Always say thanks, and that's it."

"That sounds easy enough."

"It is. The only challenge is when a lot of people are in the store at once."

I looked outside, towards the building where I lived. "I've walked by this place so many times in the past month, and I've never seen more than one or two people here at a time."

"That's during the day. You'll be working weekend nights. That's when we get the most traffic."

"Why's that? I figured weekend nights were quiet."

"Not here." Moe said, pointing to two clubs across the street. "They're open Friday, Saturday and Sunday nights. People party all night and stop here for water, energy drinks and cigarettes. It gets crazy busy. But it's fun."

"Got it. So what else do I need to know about the store?"

"Chill, brother. We've got plenty of time to train you. Your shift doesn't start until Friday, and it's only Monday today." Moe said, leaning back casually.

We spent the next hour chatting about our lives—our childhoods, why we came to Australia. Moe lived with his mother and sister here, while I was navigating this new world with just the few friends I'd made.

Moe was studying criminal law, which impressed me, though it did make me wonder if he'd recognise that we were both working below legal wages and beyond legally allocated hours—being paid in cash. But he quickly reassured me when he mentioned he was in the same boat, working all seven days a week. It gave me some relief. If anything went wrong, at least I had a law student on my side.

Just as I was settling in, the first customer walked in. Moe sat back, signalling for me to take the lead. I greeted the man as instructed, though pleasantries weren't exactly my thing. I preferred straightforward interactions—grab what you want, pay and leave.

"Hello." I said.

"Hello." the customer replied warmly. "How are you?"

"I'm good, thanks. How about you?"

"Doing well." he said with a nod, before grabbing a bottle of water and placing it on the counter.

I scanned it. "That'll be two dollars and ninety-five cents, please."

"Card, please." he said, tapping his wallet.

I keyed in the amount on the EFTPOS machine and asked, "Would you like a receipt?"

"No, thanks."

I put the receipt in the tin, handed him his card back, and said, "Thank you, see you later."

"You, too. Have a good day." the customer said as he walked out.

"That was great." Moe said with a grin. "You picked that up quick."

"Told you, it's easy." I said, feeling a little more confident.

Moe walked me around the store, showing me where everything was. He pointed to a door in the corner.

"This is where we keep all the stock. If anything runs out on the shelves, come back here. If it's not here, note it down, and I'll restock it in the morning. Oh, and this is the CCTV screen for security."

"Is that all for security?" I asked.

"No, we've got a hammer under the counter, just in case." he said with a grin.

I raised an eyebrow, clearly unconvinced a hammer would save me in any real trouble.

Moe laughed. "Relax, man. Nothing happens here. We're in the Queen Victoria Building, and there's night security. Just remember to give them a 50 percent discount whenever they buy something, and you'll be fine."

"Got it. Hopefully, I won't need the hammer."

"Don't worry, it's safe here."

We returned to the counter and waited for a few more customers. After a couple of quiet hours, Moe said, "That's it for today. Come back tomorrow, same time."

"That's it? Nothing else to learn?"

"Tomorrow I'll show you how to clean the store. Everyone has to clean up at the end of their shift."

"Okay, see you tomorrow." I said, grabbing my bag and heading out.

As I reached the front door, Moe called after me and placed 30 dollars on the counter. "This is for today's work. Come back tomorrow, okay?"

"Wait, what? For two hours?" I asked, surprised.

"We pay for all shifts. We don't get free work here."

"Thanks." I said, feeling a strange sense of pride as I pocketed the money. It wasn't much, but it was my first pay in Australia. There's something magical about your first pay, no matter how small.

I went to my usual spot for a meal, savouring it a little more than usual, before heading straight to uni for my lecture.

The next two days followed the same routine—training for two hours, grabbing a meal, and calling my parents to update them. I always told them to keep faith, promising I'd have good news by Monday.

By Thursday, I was anxious. Would I get my first real shift on Friday? I showed up at the store at noon, as usual, but this time, Moe was nowhere to be seen. I assumed he was in the storeroom, so I headed back there. No sign of him.

"Moe? Moe?" I called out, pacing around the store. Still no answer. Then I heard a loud "Boom!" and jumped back, heart racing.

Moe appeared, crouched behind the counter, laughing his head off. "Got you!" he said, grinning ear to ear.

"You scared the hell out of me!" I was still trying to catch my breath.

"Mission accomplished." he said, still laughing. "Anyway, you don't need to come during the day anymore."

My heart sank. "Why? What did I do wrong? I need this job, Moe. If I messed up, just tell me, and I'll fix it."

"Relax, brother. Your shift starts tonight. Go home, get some sleep, and come back fresh. It's going to be a long night. Bring some books or headphones. Weekday nights are quiet—perfect for working on your assignments."

I exhaled. "You've got to stop scaring me, man. I thought I was fired!"

Moe laughed again. "I've been planning this all morning since Sam told me to get you ready for the night shifts. It's going to get busy on weekends. If I'd known you'd react like that, I would've filmed it!"

"Yeah, real funny." I said, rolling my eyes. "What time do I start tonight?"

"Ten p.m. You'll finish at eight in the morning. I'll come to relieve you."

"Got it. Thanks, Moe. I'll see you tonight." I said, heading for the door.

"See ya." he called out.

As I left, I thought about the 90 dollars I'd earned over the past three days. It wasn't much, but it felt like a lifeline. I decided to skip my lecture and rest up.

When I got home, I turned to Rounak. "Hey, let me know what they teach in class today. I won't be there—I've got work tonight."

"Congrats, man." he said with a grin.

I smiled, feeling both nervous and excited. The real test started tonight.

"It's just a pilot shift. I'll know by Monday if it's confirmed."

"Everything will be fine. Get some rest. I'll see you at the store after the lecture tonight."

"Thanks." I said, heading to my room to change into sleep-wear. It was hard to fall asleep at first—my body felt fully rested from the previous night—but my mind knew how important tonight was. Eventually, I drifted off into a solid sleep.

I woke up at 5 p.m., and was unable to fall back asleep, but I figured I'd be fresh enough for the night ahead. So I got ready for class.

"I thought you were skipping the lecture to rest up for work." Rounak said, raising an eyebrow.

"My parents are paying a lot for me to study here. I need to keep up with the coursework, even with the job."

"That's a good attitude. Plus, remember—if the university finds out you're skipping classes for work, they could report you. That's grounds for deportation."

"Seriously? I didn't know that!" I said. "Thanks for the heads-up."

Together, we left for the lecture.

The class went smoothly. I learned a few things, though whether or not they'd be useful in life was a different question. Regardless, attending kept me focused and sharpened my ability to concentrate. During class, I casually mentioned that I'd got a part-time job and that tonight would be my first shift. "If anyone's free, swing by the store to help me pass the time." I added with a smile.

Fully packed for the night, I made sure to bring my charger, phone and headphones. I hadn't eaten much on purpose, thinking hunger might help keep me awake. It wasn't the best idea, but I figured a little discomfort might sharpen my senses through the night.

When I arrived at the store, Moe was behind the counter.

"Hey, bro." I said, stepping in.

"You're here 45 minutes early." he noted.

"Yeah, finished class early, chatted with friends, and didn't want to go home just to come back. Thought I'd hang with you until my shift starts at ten."

"Good. I've been bored. Barely anyone's come in for hours, and I forgot my charger at home. So, I've had nothing to do."

"My pleasure to keep you company." I laughed.

"By the way, I'll need to show you how to do the daily settlement. It's the most important part of closing out the accounts each day. I'll walk you through it tomorrow morning."

"Is it complicated?"

"Nah, just counting cash, generating a report and filling out this sheet." He pointed to a form under the counter. "I'll teach you tomorrow, don't worry."

We chatted about the day. Moe mentioned some deliveries he'd taken in and how slow the traffic had been. After the shop talk, he shifted gears.

"Hey, bro, follow me on Facebook. I make comedy videos. I need more followers."

"Comedy videos?" I asked, intrigued.

"Yeah, just short, fun stuff. Follow my page and check out my videos during your shift tonight."

"Sure, I will."

"I'll quiz you tomorrow morning to make sure you're telling the truth." he added with a grin.

At ten sharp, Moe stood up to leave. "All right, I'm off. See you in the morning. Stay awake, stay safe and stay warm."

"Thanks, man. Good night."

After he left, I pulled out my headphones and started watching a web series on YouTube. For the first hour, customers trickled in every few minutes. Then, the night grew colder and quieter. I moved a chair closer to the heater, wrapping myself in warmth, but eventually realised I needed to move around to stay awake. I left the counter, checking the shelves and refilling stock from the storeroom.

The storeroom was warm, and I lingered there, delaying my return to the cold front of the store. Hunger finally got the best of me, so I grabbed a pie from the shelf, jotted it down, and sat back by the heater with my phone.

Soon after, a guy in a black suit, white shirt and black tie walked in—like a character straight out of a movie. It clicked: this was the security guy Moe had mentioned.

"Hey mate, how's it going?" he said, snapping me out of my thoughts.

"I'm good, just freezing." I replied, managing a smile.

"Yeah, it's brutal out here. Late August, and we're still stuck in winter." he said, shaking his head. "Are you working tomorrow, too?"

"Yep, Friday through Sunday nights."

"Ah, brace yourself. It gets wild on weekends. Drunks and people high on drugs can cause trouble. They don't know what they're doing half the time."

"Great …" I muttered, unsure how to respond.

He picked up a product, and I rang it up. "Three dollars, ninety-five cents." I said, then knew I'd made a mistake when he raised an eyebrow. "Oh, sorry! I forgot the discount. It's so cold, my brain's not working."

"No worries, bud." he chuckled.

I adjusted the price, and he paid with a smile. We chatted for a while, which helped pass the time.

At 5 a.m., the newspaper delivery guy came in, followed by the milkman. I signed for the goods, put them away, and returned to the counter.

The night dragged on, with videos and the occasional chat with the security team keeping me awake. As 8 a.m. approached, I cleaned the store, tired but relieved.

Right on time, Moe walked in. "How was the night?" he asked.

"Quiet. The whole city was asleep." I replied, yawning.

"Enjoy the calm while it lasts. The weekend's gonna be crazy. I'm telling you, we make more money in one weekend night than all the weekdays combined."

"We'll see." I said, exhausted.

I waited at the counter, expecting my pay for the night. Moe noticed and smirked. "What?"

"My pay for the shift?" I asked, hesitating. "Didn't come out right. I meant … could I get paid?"

Moe's eyes twinkled. "Didn't Sam tell you?"

"He barely talks to me."

"Well, he called this morning. You're officially hired. Permanent staff now—until something big happens, of course. He was watching the CCTV all night and was impressed with how you handled things."

"Wait, so I have a job?" I asked, surprised.

"Yep, that's what I've been trying to tell you! You're permanent now."

Relief washed over me. "Thanks, Moe. No more stress. I can finally stop worrying." Overcome with gratitude, I stepped forward and gave him a quick hug. "I'll tell my dad today."

"Go get some sleep, man." Moe laughed.

I headed home and told my roommates the good news. They cheered and demanded a party, but I promised to treat them once I got my first paycheck. After a bit of celebration, I crashed, finally letting myself rest.

Around 1 p.m., I woke briefly and called my dad. "Hello, Papa."

"Should I book your flight back to India?" he asked, skipping pleasantries as usual.

"No need. I got a part-time job."

"Great! Where?"

"At a convenience store near my place. Like a general store back home."

"And what will you be doing?"

"Cashier work, stock refills, cleaning. The shifts are long—ten hours over the weekends—but it fits perfectly with my class schedule."

"How much are they paying you?"

"Fifteen dollars an hour. Thirty hours a week, so about $450 weekly."

"Good. Manage your expenses wisely. Try to save some of your money to pay off a bit of your debt."

"Yes, Papa."

"You working nights?"

"Yes, but Melbourne's safe, and there's security around. It's a quiet job."

"All right, take care of yourself. I'll let your mum know. She's happy for you, too."

We hung up, and I drifted back into sleep, ready to face the busy weekend Moe had warned me about.

"See you guys! Drop by the store whenever—you'll get a discount on whatever you need." I said to my roommates, Vikram, Rounak and Madhur, along with their friends Mazhar and Vishal, who had come over for some fun. After they left, I had a peaceful sleep, to be fully energised for the busy night Moe had warned me about.

Stepping out of the building, I was greeted by a bustling city full of partygoers. Men in shirts and pants, no jackets, and women in short sleeveless dresses made me wonder how they weren't freezing. Even with four layers of clothing, I had to shove my hands in my jacket pockets to fend off the cold.

As I approached the store, I saw a steady flow of people going in and out. Worried something might be wrong, I quickened my pace. When I entered, I found Moe at the counter, looking completely drained. He barely noticed me as he rang up customers. It was the first time I saw just how busy the place could get.

"Hey, Moe, how's it going?" I asked as I walked behind the counter.

"You're early again. Thanks, man. We're slammed tonight—some famous DJ is playing at Two Floors Up (TFU). Everyone's rushing in early to avoid the queue."

"Need any help?"

"The store's practically empty. I haven't had a second to restock. Can you man the counter while I refill the shelves?"

"Sure, no problem."

"Appreciate it, brother." Moe said, handing me control of the counter before disappearing into the back.

It felt like the party had moved into the store. People were buying cigarettes, chewing gum, pies, soft drinks, and water—anything to keep their night going.

When Moe came back to the counter, he said, "We're going to run out of soft drinks and energy drinks before the night's over. I'll have to restock tomorrow."

"Got it. Good night, Moe. See you in the morning."

"Take care, brother."

For the next two hours, I served a steady stream of customers. By midnight, things quietened down, so I took the chance to restock the shelves.

A security guard who looked Indian walked in, and I hurried back to the counter. "Hey, how's it going?" I asked.

"Busy night with the party at TFU."

"Yeah, it's my first weekend shift." I admitted.

"Thought so. Haven't seen you around before."

I smiled. "Just started this week. I'm from India, trying to make things work here."

"Good to be independent." he said. "Immigrants from the subcontinent usually have it tough at first."

"Where are you from?" I asked.

"Peshawar, Pakistan." he said.

I hesitated, unsure how to respond. Growing up, India and Pakistan were painted as enemies, but before I could say anything, he smiled.

"Don't worry, brother. Here, it's different. We face the same challenges, and those struggles unite us. As you spend more time here, you'll see Indians and Pakistanis supporting each other."

"How long have you been here?" I ask.

"Almost ten years. I've done all kinds of jobs, but I like security work. Good pay, and there's always someone to talk to."

"That's great. Can I help you with anything? Moe said I can give you a 50 percent discount on whatever you need."

"I'm good. Just came by to check on you. The security guy from last night mentioned you were new, so I thought I'd make sure you were doing okay."

"Thanks, I appreciate that." I said, surprised by the kindness of strangers. It was humbling how much people looked out for one another.

We chatted for a while until we saw a flood of people leaving TFU. "It's about to get busy." he warned, and he was right. A steady stream of customers poured in, most of them Middle Eastern, many with wads of cash.

One tall, skinny guy approached the counter. "Hey, brother! How's your night been?"

"Busy but good. How about yours?"

"Amazing! The DJ is killer, and the club's packed with babes!" He grinned, sticking his tongue out.

I laughed. "What can I get you?"

"Three packs of Marlboro Gold, please."

"Twenties?"

"Twenty-fives."

I rang him up. "That's 90 dollars."

He pulled out a fat bundle of hundreds, peeled one off, and handed it to me. "Keep the change."

A few more customers holding wads of cash followed, who also said to keep the change. That was 45 bucks in tips. I wasn't sure what to do with it, so I set it aside and figured I'd ask Moe in the morning.

For the next two hours, I sold cigarettes and drinks to tired partygoers. By six in the morning, the streets were emptying and the shop was quiet.

As the dawn light filtered through the windows, I restocked the shelves and cleaned the store, waiting for Moe to arrive.

When he finally walked in, he smiled. "How was the night, brother? My cousin was at TFU and said you were doing a great job. Word gets back to Sam, you know."

"Thanks, man. It was busy, but the time flew by."

"Time flies when you're having fun." he chuckled. As I packed up to leave, he paused, noticing the pile of cash I'd set aside. "What's with the cash?"

"Tips. I didn't know what to do with it, so I left it here."

Moe grinned. "That's yours, brother. Keep it."

With $100 in tips, I left the store feeling pretty good. The next two nights went by fast—Saturday was chaotic, but Sunday was calm. By Monday morning, I was paid 600 dollars. The first thing on my mind? A good meal. I Googled the best Indian food in Melbourne and found a place called Red Carpet, just around the corner from home.

I woke up in the afternoon and stepped out of my room, finding only Vikram at home. "Where is everyone?" I asked.

"Rounak's at work, and Madhur's at uni." Vikram replied.

"What about Mazhar and Vishal? I've seen them around but haven't had the chance to introduce myself."

"They're back at their place."

I nodded, feeling the pangs of hunger hit. "I'm starving. I can't wait for them. Wanna join me at Red Carpet? My treat."

"Yeah, sure." he said, getting ready in no time.

Within minutes, we were digging into some delicious food. We ate quickly, barely talking, and were back home within an hour. I crashed again, hoping to catch some more sleep before my lecture.

The next few weeks passed peacefully, filled with a rhythm of meeting new people, making friends, working, studying, and finishing assignments.

One day, while on the tram to university, I greeted a man sitting across me with a smile, and he responded with the same.

"Hello." he said.

"Hi." I replied. Ever since starting my part-time job, I'd become better at small talk.

"How are you?"

"I'm good, thanks. How about you?"

"Good. You studying here?" he asked, and I nodded. "Where are you from originally?"

"Mumbai, India. I came here a couple of months ago. Always wanted to be in Australia, and now that I'm here, it feels great. Still, a long way to go, though. What about you?"

"I'm Aboriginal." he said. Noticing my puzzled expression he continued, "We're the longest surviving tribe in Australia. On behalf of all Aboriginal people, welcome to our country. May you have a long and prosperous future here."

TIME FLIES AND CHANGES

Since getting the job, life had become fun, and many of my friends started asking if there were openings at the store. Whenever someone was looking for work, I'd call Sam to see if he had any leads. His response was always the same: "We'll keep their details on file and reach out when needed."

One evening, I called him again. "Hey, Sam. How's it going?"

"Good, mate. What's up?" His down-to-earth vibe always put me at ease.

"My classmate Govind is looking for a job. Just wanted to let you know."

"Great timing. The guy who works weekday nights is leaving, so we'll need someone to fill in. I was actually going to call you about it tonight."

"Perfect. Govind's keen to take those shifts."

"Good to hear. Bring him along for a few nights while you work, and I'll meet him after that. His pay will be the same as yours, so make sure he's okay with that."

"Got it. Thanks, Sam. Talk soon."

I hung up and turned to Govind. "Good news, mate. We've got an opening. You'll start by shadowing me on weekend nights for a couple of weeks, and then Sam will take it from there."

"That's amazing. Thanks, man. I really appreciate it." His excitement was contagious, and it felt great to help a friend.

Life carried on smoothly with a mix of studying and work. With a steady pay, I was in a good place. Some nights at the store were particularly fun. People enjoyed chatting with me, and a few regulars even stopped by just to say hi on their way to a party. They often came back later in the night, buzzed and grateful for small discounts.

One night, I witnessed a fight between bouncers and some partygoers outside the store. On another occasion, the police arrested a group of people for vandalising city property. There were even nights when ambulances showed up, cutting the party short. It was eye-opening to see how wild things could get with just alcohol.

One night, the usual crowd was trickling in and out of the store. Three girls, regulars I'd got to know, walked in. They were dressed to the nines, as always.

"Hey girls, how's it going tonight?" I asked.

"We're great! How about you?" one of them responded.

"Busy as usual, but all good. I've got an assignment due on Monday, though, so I'll probably start working on that once things quieten down after six."

"Fun." said the second girl, flashing a smile.

"You should come party with us one of these nights." the first one teased.

"I wish! But I'm stuck working weekend nights. Maybe if I get a night off, I'll join you. I'm sure I'll find you all there." I said.

After some small talk, they left, and their flirty banter kept me smiling through the night.

Another evening, I was chatting with the Pakistani security guard when two blonde girls stumbled into the store. They could barely walk straight. After some effort, they brought a bottle of water to the counter.

"How's your night going?" I asked, already guessing the answer.

"Too many MDs tonight." one of them slurred.

"MDs?"

"It's a drug, MDMA. Keeps you going all night." she said, still struggling with her words. "We took two each and have been jumping ever since. Needed some fresh air and water before heading back."

"Sounds like quite the night." I said, handing over the water.

As they were leaving, one of the blondes turned back and asked, "Can I ask you something?"

"Sure, what is it?"

"Do you have a bomb?" she asked, completely serious. Her friend, realising how offensive that sounded, quickly apologised and scolded her for asking.

The drunk one persisted, though. "Come on, do you?"

I glanced at the security guard and replied, "Yeah, I had two. Lost one yesterday, so be careful when you're walking around."

Stunned by my response, they left with a mix of confusion and embarrassment.

"Nice comeback." the security guard said, chuckling. "We need to respond to racist comments like that more often."

I nodded in agreement. "Yeah, it's the only way to make them think twice."

"Very true."

We continued chatting, and I mention, "The guy who works here on weekdays had a situation last week."

"Oh? What happened?"

"Some girl asked for free chewing gum. When he refused, she flashed him in exchange for it. He called me yesterday, laughing about it. Some nights here are just wild."

"It's definitely the drugs. Things have been rough for security lately. Just a couple of weeks ago, one of the guys got attacked by a group of drunks with a beer bottle. The police are involved now, and they're cracking down. If this keeps up, these clubs might get shut down."

"And when they close, this shop will, too." I said, and we both laughed.

———∞∞∞———

With money coming in steadily and my savings growing, I started missing my family. I especially wanted to be home for Amar's birthday. One afternoon, Mazhar suggested I book tickets to India and visit my family, rather than just missing them from afar. After checking ticket prices, I found February was the off-peak season and pretty cheap. Without thinking twice, I booked my flight.

As soon as I had the confirmation, I called home. "Hey, Mum. I'm coming home in February for Amar's birthday!"

"Why so soon? You've only been gone a few months. You should be saving your money for the future, not spending it on unnecessary trips." she scolded, her usual frugality kicking in.

I sighed, knowing I couldn't change her mind. "I've already booked the tickets, Mum. No backing out now."

I didn't tell her the real reason for coming back so soon—that I hadn't been able to fully enjoy my time with them before I left. Now, with no financial stress, I just wanted to relax and spend quality time with my family, free from worries.

———∞∞∞———

One afternoon, I woke up feeling refreshed and stepped out to see everyone sitting together, enjoying lunch.

"How was your sleep, Charmander?" Vikram asked.

"Why do you call him Charmander? Is it because of how he looks?" Vishal asked with a sly grin.

"No, it's because he's always full of energy—like his tail is on fire." Vikram joked. "He's booking the MCG tour for Sunday. The guy works both Saturday and Sunday nights. How he's going to manage that, I have no idea. But if anyone can, it's him."

I laughed and asked, "Anyone want to join me for the tour? It's free."

"What time is it?" Rounak asked.

"It's an all-day event, but I'll head there right after my shift at nine."

"That's too early for us." he replied, half-smiling.

"I'll share the link in the group. If you change your mind, book it." I said, trying to convince them.

"Who else is going with you?"

"Govind and Mazhar. They're both interested."

Two weeks later, the MCG Open Day finally arrived, and I was beyond excited. After a busy Saturday night shift, I called Govind. "Hey buddy, you up?"

"Yeah, almost ready to go." he replied, sounding fresh.

"Cool. I'm going to wake Mazhar. See you at my building at 8:45."

"Got it. See you soon."

I rushed home, woke Mazhar, and we got ready. The three of us met on time and headed to Parliament Station. I had a Red Bull before leaving, so I was full of energy, literally, running towards the station.

As we boarded the train, Mazhar looked at me, surprised. "You worked all night, and you're still bouncing around."

"Sometimes it's just the Red Bull." I said, grinning.

Before long, we'd reached Richmond station. We got off and walked to the MCG. The atmosphere was electric—music thumped through the air and sports-themed props lined the entrance. As soon as we entered, the vastness of the stadium hit us. The sheer scale of it, combined with the history embedded in its walls, gave us all a thrill. There were families, sports enthusiasts and tourists everywhere, all eager to explore this iconic place.

We spotted stalls for footy and cricket. One booth had a speed gun to measure bowling pace. People were bowling, men hitting around 120 km/h and women about 80. Govind went first and clocked 105. When my turn came, I bowled a disappointing 68.

Mazhar couldn't help himself. "You bowl slower than the girls around here." he teased.

"Red Bull gives WIIIIINGS, not pace." I said. "Why don't you try, tough guy?"

"My shoulders hurt." Mazhar dodged, pretending to rub his arm.

We wandered around the stadium, admiring statues of Shane Warne, Dennis Lillee, Don Bradman and other Australian cricket legends. After snapping photos with the statues, we got a warm welcome from the MCG staff, who handed us maps and a schedule.

Our first stop was the National Sports Museum inside the stadium, a treasure trove of Australian sports history. We marvelled at glittering trophies, vintage cricket bats and interactive exhibits. Each corner of the museum told stories of Australia's rich sporting past—Cricket World Cups, AFL Grand Finals, and the 1956 Olympic Games.

In the museum, I struck a pose beside Don Bradman's statue, trying to mimic his batting stance for the camera. We were also excited to see the World Cup trophies on display, and we clicked plenty of photos.

Next came the guided tour of the MCG itself. The guides were knowledgeable, long-time members of the MCG community, and their insider stories brought the stadium to life. We walked through the players' changing rooms, where we could almost feel the pre-match jitters. The Long Room, with its prestigious decor and portraits of cricketing legends, gave us a glimpse into the world of MCC (Melbourne Cricket Club) members.

The highlight of the day was stepping onto the lush green turf of the MCG itself. Standing at the centre of the pitch, I felt a rush of awe. This was the same ground where countless legends had played, where records were made, and where history had been written. The panoramic view from the centre was breathtaking, giving us a sense of the stadium's immense scale.

We also visited the media centre, sitting in the same seats used by commentators and journalists from all over the world. It was fascinating to see how global broadcasts are produced and how much effort goes into making events at the MCG run smoothly.

Throughout the day, there were plenty of interactive activities. Kids were practising in cricket clinics, coached by professionals, and there were face-painting stalls and photo opportunities with mascots.

As we roamed through the stadium, I noticed generations of fans sharing stories and making new memories. The sense of camaraderie was contagious, and it was easy to see why the MCG is called the heart of Melbourne. We sat in the stands, taking it all in.

"I've been to Wankhede, and it looks so small compared to this." I said, still amazed by the scale.

"Well, this *is* the largest cricket ground." Govind replied.

"Thank you for the information." I said, with a sarcastic smile.

As we admired the stadium, we noticed the sky darkening with clouds. Just when we were about to complain about the weather ruining the perfect day, the MCG lights turned on, casting a magical glow over the grounds. Everyone, including us, stayed a little longer, soaking in the atmosphere and taking in one last look at the iconic stands.

The MCG Open Day wasn't just a tour—it was an immersive experience that celebrated the spirit of sport, the joy of community and the rich legacy of one of the world's greatest stadiums. It left me with a deeper appreciation for the MCG and the countless historic moments it's hosted over the years.

After a couple of hours, I started feeling the exhaustion hit me. Knowing I had to work another night shift, I decided to head back early. I left Govind and Mazhar at the MCG, still admiring the place, and went home. After a good nap, I was ready for another shift at work.

———◦◇◇◇◦———

"Our lease ends in two months. We need to start looking for our next place." Rounak said, a couple of weeks after our MCG tour.

I was still riding the high from that experience. "There's too much partying here. I need to move somewhere quieter, focus on studies and work."

"I was thinking the same." Rounak replied. "Should we move in together?"

"Let's ask Mazhar, too. It'll be tough telling everyone, but I think it's for the best."

Later that day, when everyone was watching TV, I asked Mazhar if he wanted to join me and Rounak in finding a new place. He agreed without hesitation. Then came the hard part—I had to tell the rest of the group. I've never been good at breaking bad news; I prefer being the bearer of good news. One of these days, to work on myself, I'll have to practise delivering bad news.

"No way." Mazhar shot back when I asked him to do it for me. "It's your idea. You tell them."

Rounak also flat-out refused. I was on my own.

I thought about ways to delegate the task, but knew they were all my friends, too. I didn't want to be the reason anyone got upset. So, I devised a plan. I went up to Mazhar and Rounak.

"Mazhar, you'll be heading back to Bangladesh as soon as the semester break starts, right?"

He nodded.

"And Rounak, you'll be working every day during the break?"

Another nod.

"Here's the thing." I began, "I found out that renting a new place isn't as easy as it seems. We can't just apply online. First, we have to find properties on apps such as Realestate or Domain, but then we need to attend inspections in person."

"What? We can't just apply?" Mazhar asked, confused.

"Nope. We have to attend the inspections, and they usually last about 15 minutes. If we like the place, we can apply, but we'll need to provide identification, employment details, and our rental history."

"Our bank details and rental history are solid." Rounak added.

"True, but I'm the only one who can go to these inspections since both of you will be busy." I said. Then, turning to Mazhar, "So, what can you do in all this?"

He thought hard, squinting at me, rubbing his teeth, but didn't have an answer.

"So, you'll be the one to tell everyone the plan." I concluded.

Mazhar knew where this was heading. His eyes narrowed as he tried to think of an escape but found none.

Later, when we were all gathered, Mazhar spoke up. "Jaideep, Rounak and I have decided that after this lease ends, we'll find an apartment for ourselves."

He threw us under the bus, but no one seemed bothered. Everyone just carried on with their day. It was smoother than I had anticipated. Soon after, I found out that everyone else was also planning to move out and find places with other friends.

Life settled into a rhythm. Uni was going well, and I managed to score high distinctions in all my subjects in the first semester. Feeling like I was off to a great start with my master's, I thought the rest would be smooth sailing.

Working weekend nights meant I got paid on Mondays, which turned into party nights for me. I'd stop by Dan Murphy's before my Monday evening lecture, grab some drinks, and take them to class. After all, the lecture ended at nine, and Dan Murphy's closed at seven, so better to be safe than sorry. My choice of alcohol depended on how much I made in tips over the weekend. My friends loved the mid-week party vibe, too.

After the first semester, we had a four-month break. With nothing to fill my time, I Googled ways to keep busy. The search suggested reading, so I decided to give it a shot. I picked up an autobiography by Kevin Pietersen, a South African-born English cricketer. The book was so gripping that I finished it in three days. Then I bought another cricket autobiography and finished that in four days. I was devouring books faster than I expected, but spending too much money on them. I needed a hobby that would pass the time and make me money.

That's when I discovered online betting. Bet365 was offering a sign-up bonus, so I joined with 50 dollars and got another 50 as a bonus. The app was easy to use, and I started small, betting 50 cents on each ball of a test match between Australia and New Zealand. I bet on "no run" for each ball, and surprisingly, it worked. After a few hours, I was up ten dollars. By the end of the five-day match, I had made 19 dollars. I withdrew my initial 50 and left the bonus money in the account, aiming to someday turn it into millions.

"With my reliance on Dan Murphy's and Bet365, I should probably become a member of both and enjoy some perks." I joked to Vikram.

"Dan Murphy's is a good idea. Members get discounts. But what are you going to do with a Bet365 membership?" he asked.

"Membership is free, and it's a fun way to pass time. We've watched enough cricket to predict things accurately about 60 percent of the time. Sixty percent is pretty good."

"Then go for it." Vikram said, shrugging.

A few days later, I checked the letterbox and found my membership letters from both places. I brought them home and placed them on the table. "Mum and Dad would be so proud." Rounak joked after seeing the letters, and everyone burst into laughter.

Despite our jokes and growing friendships, it was a shame that we'd be living apart after two months, as per our decision.

———◦◦◇◦◦———

I'm an engineer by choice, and I've always liked making things. So, when I learned how to roll my own cigarettes, it became another small project. I'd roll a few and leave them on the table for anyone to grab. It wasn't much, but it gave me something to focus on, a little routine.

One evening, as I sat reading, betting on the cricket and rolling cigarettes all at once, the door opened, and in walked a girl. She was a mutual friend, followed by a few others, but the moment I saw her, the world slowed down. I was completely caught off guard, too stunned to even process the fact that there was a party about to happen in our apartment.

"So, you ready for the party?" someone patted me on the back, pulling me out of my daze.

"Yeah, totally." I muttered. But in my head, I was screaming, *Introduce me to her!*

As the evening unfolded, with people coming and going, my mind stayed locked on her. The problem was, I didn't know how to approach her. Should I just say hi?

But so many people had already said hi to her. It had to be something different, something memorable. I hovered nearby, trying to catch bits of conversation, hoping to figure out what she was into. But before I could manufacture a decent opening line, she was already leaving.

No, don't go, I thought as I watched her head for the door.

"You were awfully quiet today." Vishal said, catching me off guard. "Everything okay?"

"Yeah, just wasn't feeling the vibe tonight."

"Right. You were completely fixated on that girl, weren't you?" he smirked.

"What? No way." But inside, I was panicking. Was it that obvious? Did she notice, too?

"Plenty of people are into her." Madhur said. "If you're serious, you better act fast, or someone else will."

"There's nothing to act on. Sure, I liked her, but I like a lot of girls, daily. Ask me tomorrow, and I probably won't even remember her."

But that night, even after the music, the laughs, and the drinks, she was all I could think about. I didn't even know her name, then, and asking for it would've been too obvious, so I stayed quiet, waiting for a better opportunity. Eventually, we all called it a night. Except sleep wasn't coming easy for me. My mind was full of her, and no matter how hard I tried, I couldn't shake the thought of her.

The next morning, she was still there—firmly lodged in my mind. I couldn't help myself; I started looking for her on Facebook. But without a name, it was impossible to find her. Frustrated, I tried meditating to clear my head, but it only made her presence in my mind more pronounced. The more I tried to push her away, the more she took over, and soon, she wasn't just in my thoughts—she had moved into my heart, too.

Every time the doorbell rang, I hoped it was her. Every time I gambled, I thought of her. Rolling cigarettes? Thinking of her. Drinking? Yep, her again. It was driving me insane. I had goals, a life to focus on and yet here I was, distracted by someone who was probably already in a relationship. I needed closure.

"I can't stop thinking about her." I finally admitted to Madhur as we headed to the gym.

"Don't do this to yourself, man. She's gone. Move on. I've noticed you've changed a lot since you saw her."

"I didn't even meet her, I just stared at her."

"Well, whatever you call it, it's changed you. People like being around you because you're always smiling. That's what makes you *you*. But ever since that night, you've been a lot quieter, like the rest of us boring folk."

"I know. My life was going great, and now it feels like this is dragging me down. Usually, if I like a girl and she doesn't like me back, I move on. Same if a girl likes me and I'm not into her. But this feels different. I almost wish she'd reject me just so I could have some closure."

"What can I do to help?"

"Well … What's her name?"

Madhur told me her full name: Sapna Sharma, and I immediately searched for her again on Facebook. Dozens of profiles came up.

"I can't find her." I complained.

"Go through my profile. She's on my friend list."

Voila! I found her and sent a friend request. Before stalking her profile, I noticed her last picture was with a guy.

"Who's this guy?" I asked.

"How would I know?"

"Good point. But are all the guys in her photos the same?" I asked, scrolling through her pictures.

"Doesn't matter. She's not going to be with you."

"I know. I just need closure."

"She takes forever to accept friend requests anyway. She accepted mine because we met in the library, and I sent it right there. She doesn't even know you. Yours will probably be ignored like all the others."

My phone pinged. "She just accepted it." I said, grinning. I started dancing in the street, proving Madhur wrong.

We started online chatting soon after, at the gym. I was on the treadmill, but instead of running, I was walking so I could focus on our conversation.

"Do you like cycling?" she asked, after the small talk fizzled out.

"I love it. When I was in India, I had a scooter, but I used to trade it with friends who had bicycles just to ride them."

"Nice. I live in St Kilda, and there are great places to cycle here. The house I'm staying at has a bunch of bikes, but I can never find anyone to ride with. Would you like to join me?"

Yes. A thousand times yes, I thought. But instead, I calmly replied, "I'd love to."

"How about Saturday morning?"

"I work Friday, Saturday, and Sunday nights. Can we do Tuesday, Wednesday, or Thursday instead?"

"How about tomorrow? It's Thursday."

"Perfect. Where should I meet you?"

"Get off at the Esplanade tram stop, and I'll meet you there at eight."

I got home dancing and smiling, my mood impossible to miss. Everyone noticed immediately that something good had happened. I proudly showed them the chat, then cracked open a bottle of Red Label. They all cheered, but deep down, they were mostly waiting for me to get rejected— just another casualty— and nurse another broken heart. This was the calm before the storm, and everyone drank to it.

That night, I went to bed early, knowing I had to be at St Kilda by eight. I slept like a baby and woke up on time, feeling fresh and ready. Vikram was up when I was about to leave.

"Call me first when she stomps on your heart." he said with a grin.

"Why are you so sure that's going to happen? We're just cycling today."

"No, you're cycling because her boyfriend doesn't like it, and he's not worried about her hanging out with you. You'll go for a ride, have a good time, and just when things are going well, her boyfriend will show up, kiss her in front of you, and take her away."

"Thanks for the vivid mental image." I shot back, flipping him the bird.

He laughed, and before he could continue, I was out the door. I stopped by the store and met Govind on the way. I told him the whole story, and he was excited for me, too. I grabbed a Red Bull and an orange juice for the ride and hopped on the tram to the Esplanade. I got there right at eight and called her. No answer.

The soft morning light bathed the city as I stepped off the tram, my heart racing. St Kilda had this old-world charm, and the fresh sea breeze mingled with the smell of coffee drifting from nearby cafes. The streets were alive with people rushing to work, lost in their own worlds, as trams rolled by, their bells echoing through the air.

So I started exploring, soaking in the architecture and the laid-back vibe. There were street performers, small bookstores and couples laughing over breakfast at outdoor cafes. As I walked, I felt less anxious. The more I wandered, the more I forgot about why I was there in the first place. St Kilda was beautiful—clear blue skies, sparkling water and golden sand. It was one of those rare occasions when all the clichés turned out to be true.

It wasn't until it was almost quarter past nine that I remembered her. I called her again. Still no answer. By then, I figured this was the end of our story. So, I decided to make the most of my time, enjoying the sights.

Just as I was strolling down the street, my phone rang. My heart leapt, thinking it was her. But it wasn't—it was Vikram.

"What's up, bro? How's the cycling going? I thought by now her boyfriend would've shown up and taken her away."

"Why do you always assume that?" I asked, exasperated.

"Because we know you."

"Okay, listen. None of that happened. She stood me up. It's been more than an hour, and she hasn't answered any of my calls."

I could hear loud laughter on the other end. Clearly, the whole crew was in on the call.

"So, what are you doing in St Kilda?" Vishal asked, still laughing.

"Honestly, just wandering around. It's beautiful here—the sky, the water, the sand. It all sounds like a cliché, but it's true. I've never seen anything like it. We should all come here sometime."

"And how long are you planning to wait?"

"I'm done waiting. I can't stand impunctuality. I'm over her now. I found the closure I was looking for. The next tram is in seven minutes, and I'm heading back home."

"We'll be ready with some drinks to help you forget." Vikram said.

"See you soon." I replied.

I was standing, waiting for the next tram, when my phone rang again. I figured it was Vikram calling to ask me to pick something up, so I ignored it. Then it rang again, and I did the same. Just as the second call ended, a text message came through. It was from her.

"Good morning! Sorry, couldn't wake up in time. Just got up. Tried calling you but couldn't connect. Call me back when you can."

I quickly called her. "Hey, Jaideep here. Just saw your text. When you called, I was on the phone with a friend, so it didn't connect." I said, trying to sound casual.

"You don't need to say your name when you call me again." she replied with a slight laugh. "Sorry for leaving you hanging. I overslept. Where are you now? I saw your call earlier at eight."

"Oh, that? I woke up early and thought about rescheduling, but I couldn't sleep, so I called a friend who lives near St Kilda. I'm on my way to meet him now."

"Okay. I'll send you my address. Come here, and we'll grab the bikes from my place."

She totally ignored my imaginary friend. "Sure, I'll cancel on him and be there in 20 minutes."

"See you soon."

I hung up and immediately called Vikram. I recounted the whole conversation to him and the others.

"You idiot." he laughed. "After we hung up, Madhur called Priyanka. Priyanka is Sapna's roommate. We told Priyanka that you'd been waiting since eight. She knows, you fool!"

"Motherf—why didn't you tell me earlier?!"

"That's why I was calling—to tell you to stay put."

I had no comeback. They did call me, and I'd ignored it.

"Did you leave already?" Vishal asked.

"No, I'm still here. She just sent me her address, and I'm heading to her place now."

"Man, what a shameful visit." Vikram teased.

"When I feel uncomfortable, I act confident." I said. "I'll keep my story straight and won't show any weakness. Let her think whatever she wants, but I won't let it affect me."

"Good luck with that, dude." Vishal chuckled, and we hung up.

I reached her place and without saying a word, we got on our bikes with our helmets on. As the sun rose over Melbourne, the sky transformed into a brilliant blue, promising a perfect day for a cycling adventure. At ten a.m., the weather was ideal, with the sun shining brightly and a gentle breeze whispering through the trees. St Kilda, renowned for its vibrant beach and bustling esplanade, was the starting point for our ride.

We started from the iconic Luna Park, its whimsical facade smiling down at us as we pedalled past. The air was filled with a sense of freedom and excitement. Families, tourists and locals were already enjoying the day, adding to the lively atmosphere. We took the bike path that runs parallel to the beach, feeling the smooth rhythm of the ride as we matched our pace with the gentle waves crashing on the shore. The palm trees lining the path swayed slightly in the breeze, casting dappled shadows on the ground.

As we rode further, we encountered a group of fellow cyclists, all greeting each other with friendly nods and smiles. The camaraderie among cyclists was palpable, creating a sense of community even among strangers. All strangers were looking more at her than at us. They couldn't believe what a girl like her was doing with a guy like me. I still didn't say anything to break the awkwardness. I kept quiet for her to apologise, as she was at fault for not being punctual. Until she did, I decided not to break the silence.

We continued on our ride; the esplanade was bustling with activity. People were jogging, walking their dogs and enjoying leisurely strolls. Cafes and restaurants were open, with outdoor seating areas filled with patrons savouring their morning coffee and breakfast. The aroma of fresh coffee and baked goods wafted through the air, tempting me to stop, but we continued to ride, determined to make the most of the beautiful morning and not say the first word.

We cycled past the St Kilda Pier, where fishermen were casting their lines and hoping for a good catch. The view from the pier was stunning, with the city skyline in the distance and sailboats dotting the sparkling water. We paused to take it all in. We got off our bikes and sat there. I removed some Red Bull and orange juice from my bag and asked her to choose. She opted for orange juice. We still hadn't said a word but were feeling grateful for the beauty of the day and the joy of cycling.

Continuing along the Bay Trail, we reached the St Kilda Marina, where sleek yachts were moored, their masts gently swaying. The path became less crowded as we ventured further, allowing us to pick up speed and enjoy the thrill of the ride. The breeze against our face was refreshing, and the sound of the waves provided a soothing soundtrack to our journey.

Eventually, we looped back towards the starting point, feeling invigorated and content. The ride had been a perfect blend of exercise, relaxation and appreciation of the natural beauty and vibrant life of St Kilda. As I dismounted my bike and stretched, I knew that this sunny Thursday morning ride would be a cherished memory, a testament to the simple pleasures of cycling in such a picturesque setting.

"Sorry to keep you waiting." she finally said as I stretched.

"No problem." I replied nonchalantly, as if nothing had happened. "Thanks for inviting me. It was an amazing experience. I've never done anything like this before."

Just as I was enjoying the feeling of relaxation, my phone buzzed—Vikram again. I declined the call, knowing full well what he wanted to ask. I wanted to know, too: did she have a boyfriend or not?

I was just about to ask her when she said, "Want to grab a coffee?"

"I just had a Red Bull. That's enough caffeine for me right now. But I'll get a juice or something. Know a good place?"

"There's coffee everywhere here. It's Melbourne."

"True. Same in the city."

We grabbed our drinks and found a bench near the beach. The sea breeze mixed with the aroma of coffee, creating the perfect atmosphere as we settled in.

"So, how have things been going for you lately?" she asked.

"Nothing much happening right now." I shrugged. "Finished my first semester with an HD (high distinction), so I'm feeling good about the rest of my master's. I work nights, though, so my sleep schedule is a mess. It's tough to find other jobs with that kind of schedule, so I've mostly been reading to pass the time. How about you?"

"I did well, too—got an HD in my first semester. But now I've got four months off and no idea what to do with myself. I've been looking for a job, but it's tough."

"Yeah, I struggled to find mine."

"Our lease is ending soon. Priyanka and I are thinking about moving to the city, where you guys live, but it's expensive."

"We're moving, too." I said.

"Really? Why?"

Why does she care? I thought, but I answered anyway.

"Too many parties. It's fun, but I can't get any work done at home. I have to go to uni to finish my assignments. With my sleep schedule, I can only really work at night, but I'm sick of the night library, so Rounak, Mazhar and I are looking for a new place."

"That makes sense now."

"What does?"

"Madhur asked Priyanka if he could move in with us. He'd take one room, and Priyanka and I would share the other. It would make it more affordable, and we'd be in the city."

"Nice. How's the apartment search going?"

"Not great. We've done a few inspections but got rejected from all of them. How about you?"

"Same. We've been rejected from more than 20 places. Every inspection is packed, and we never get priority."

"I have an idea that could solve both our problems." she said, her eyes lighting up.

"What's that?"

"Move in with us."

"What?" I asked, not sure if I'd heard her right.

"Yeah. You, your friends and us—together, we'd only need to find two apartments instead of four."

I hesitated. Should I say yes? What if her boyfriend comes over and things get complicated?

Noticing my confusion, she added, "You don't have to decide now. Think about it. It would make everything easier for all of us. I'm sure Rounak and Mazhar would agree."

"I wasn't worried about that." I said, though my mind was racing. "But yeah, it's something to think about."

"Then what were you thinking about?" she asked.

I hesitated, unsure how to phrase it, then blurting out, "What about your boyfriend?"

She shot me a look that said, *None of your business,* but replied calmly, "I don't have one. I've dated four guys in the past, but I'm single now."

I wasn't sure if I should be happy or not. Did I have a chance? If I did, should I take it? Probably.

She began with a steady voice, "Look, I know about this morning. I also know that you like me." She paused, letting the words linger between us.

"And?"

"You're not my type. Nothing will happen between us. But we can be good friends. Let's keep it that way; it will make our lives much easier."

"Okay." I replied, my voice barely above a whisper.

She smiled faintly. "Should we go for a walk on the beach? It's a good day, and this awkwardness will fade after a bit of casual interaction."

"Sure."

We started walking towards the beach. My mind was in chaos. Her words played on repeat, louder than the sound of the waves. I couldn't hear anything else, couldn't feel anything else. All I wanted was to retreat to the comfort of people who might stay longer in my life than her. Yet, a part of me clung to the moment, knowing it might be the last time we'd share this time together.

As I wrestled with my thoughts, she slipped on a patch of wet sand. Instinctively, I grabbed her hand, stopping her fall. Neither of us let go. We continued walking, fingers entwined. The connection felt surreal, and my thoughts spiralled.

What did this mean? Was her rejection just a test? If she truly meant what she said, why wasn't she pulling away?

Time blurred as my mind raced. I had braced for closure, for her boyfriend to show up and for me to walk away. But none of that happened. Instead, here we were, and I wasn't prepared for any of it.

"I'm holding your hand." I said, more to myself than to her.

"I know." she replied. "I want it, too. Without my will, this wouldn't be happening. It's … nice, isn't it?"

"What is?"

"Having someone to do the things you enjoy with. I've been alone for so long. No one's ever wanted to join me for a walk on the beach or a bike ride. Everyone complains about the weather being too cold, too hot or too windy. But you … you just came along, and I've had my best day in Australia so far."

"I do enjoy those things." I said, "but today wasn't about that. I came for you. And you just confirmed that nothing can ever happen between us."

"Yes, let's keep it casual. We'll enjoy the time we have and part ways when the time comes."

Her words stung, but her hand still held mine, and her warmth complicated my resolve.

"Is it really that easy for you?" I asked. "To dismiss all the good things coming your way because of something bad from the past?"

She stopped walking, considering my words. "No, it's not right." she admitted. "But you're pushing now, and it's ruining the day. Let's leave it here for now. We'll meet in a few days and take it forward."

"How can we 'take forward' something that you said can never happen?" I countered, using air quotes.

"Let's not talk anymore." she said firmly. "We had a good day. Don't spoil it. The tram stop's just over there. Let's walk to it, and we'll meet next week."

"I can't meet for the next four days because of work."

"I'll be in the city for an inspection on Tuesday. Let's catch up then."

I nodded and turned towards the tram stop. She tightened her grip on my hand and leaned her head on my arm as we walked. I stayed silent. If this was the last moment we'd share, I'd let it be.

As we reached the tram stop, I said, "Thanks for today. It was a good day. Let's catch up next week." I went in for a goodbye hug. She hugged me back and kissed my cheek. Stunned, I boarded the waiting tram without reacting, waving at her as it pulled away.

On the way home, I replayed the day's events, searching for clarity. I couldn't face the questions waiting for me at home, questions I didn't have answers for. So I decided to head to the library and distract myself with apartment hunting.

As I browsed, someone tapped my shoulder. "Hey, we were all worried about you. Why aren't you answering your calls?" Rounak asked.

"I'm worried about myself, too." I said. "I'm ignoring everyone's calls."

"So, you broke up already?" he laughed, clearly amused by my predicament.

"It's the opposite. We're in a casual relationship. I don't even know what that means."

Rounak Googled the term *casual relationship* and smirked. "That means she's free to date anyone, and you'll be stuck pining after her. Not just because of her, but because of who and how you are."

Friends are the strangest creatures. They mean well, but sometimes deliver their wisdom with biting sarcasm.

"Let's change the topic." I said. "I don't think we'll find an apartment before our lease ends. We might have to extend it."

"Why? What happened?"

"I've been to so many inspections. Everywhere, there are too many applicants, and they all get preference. We've been rejected from every place so far."

"Let me see if I can find something." Rounak offered.

And just like that, the conversation shifted, but my thoughts remained with Sapna, tangled in the emotions of the day.

The next couple of weeks were a blur of inspections, applications and rejection emails. I was barely keeping it together. Ignoring her, although hard, had become second nature, but it didn't make anything easier. My mind was scattered and it seemed like peace only came when I wasn't thinking about her.

Mazhar had left for Bangladesh to be with his family, and Rounak was working all day. Meanwhile, I was stuck in limbo, failing to find us a place. With every failed inspection, the pressure mounted. No help. No place to go. And the deadline was closing in.

One afternoon, Madhur called. "Sapna, Priyanka and I just secured a two-bedroom in Carlton." he said. "It's close to the city, and there's a tram stop right in front of the building. How's your search going?"

"Nowhere." I admitted. "I don't know what to do."

"My suggestion? Move in with us. We can share a room, and the girls can share the other."

"You know my situation, right? It's complicated. I don't know if I can do that."

Madhur sighed. "You're running out of time, man. You don't have a place, and finding one in a week is almost impossible. This way, you get a roof over your head, and I get some company. Besides, I spoke to Sapna. She said nothing's ever going to happen between you two. You need to stop thinking about her and be practical. In this one-sided relationship, you'll be the casualty."

"I wish it was that simple." I muttered.

Not long after, my phone buzzed again. This time, it was Sapna.

"Hello?" I answered, my tone indifferent, as though I hadn't recognised the number.

"Hi." she said. "Madhur asked me to talk to you about the apartment. Move in with us. It'll be good. We'll be together in the city, and you'll finally have a place. You're still searching, and we've already got something. It's a win for all of us."

I hesitated, my mind racing with everything that had been said. Finally, I sighed.

"Okay. I'm tired of all the rejections. I'll move in. And thanks."

TURNING POINT

"What time are you heading out?" Vikram asked as I woke up.

"Around noon, I guess. The lease starts today, so I might as well get settled in. Madhur's already there. When are you guys moving?"

"Our lease kicks in three days from now, so we'll start vacating then." he replied.

"Let me know when you start. I'll swing by to clean up before handing the keys over to the agency."

Vikram chuckled. "Of course, we'll need you to clean. You've lived here the longest, except for the past month when you've been busy with your girl ... or thinking about her, and nowhere to be found. You should've moved in with us. Now, you're in a one-sided mess, and you're going to need us more than ever. Just come over whenever you need to."

"I'm heading to India in two weeks. Once I'm there, everything will sort itself out—family, friends. I'll come back refreshed."

We exchanged a few more words, then I packed up, hugged everyone goodbye and booked an Uber. Within minutes, I was on my way to the new place, moving in with Madhur, Priyanka, and, well ... *her*.

When I arrived, I called Madhur to let me in.

"Welcome to our humble abode!" Priyanka greeted me.

"Good to be here." I smiled.

"Did you bring everything from your old place?" she asked.

"Yeah, just the two check-in bags I brought from India and my backpack."

"Backpack?" she glanced at me curiously. "Where's your backpack?"

I froze. "On my—" I turned to check. "Oh no ... I left it in the Uber."

Priyanka laughed. "You left your backpack in the car? What's going on with you?"

I quickly called the driver, hoping he hadn't driven too far. "It has my laptop in it ... "

When I finally retrieved the bag, Priyanka grinned. "So, how do you plan on surviving here, if just thinking about her makes you forget things?"

"It's simple." I said. "She may be the one I like, but cricket's the thing I love. Govind's putting together a team for the Last Man Stands league. He asked if I wanted to join, so I'll be practising during the week and playing on weekends. That should help me forget about her and focus on my life."

Madhur perked up. "Wait, what? When did this happen?"

I grinned. "Why? You interested?"

"Can I join the team, too?"

"Ask Govind. He's the captain, not me. Come to the nets with me today—it's our first day. You can meet the guys, show us what you've got. It's social cricket anyway; we're just there to have fun." I glanced at Priyanka. "This is how I'm going to get over her."

Priyanka raised an eyebrow. "You're not even under her yet. Or she is not under you."

We all laughed, though the joke stung.

Just then, Sapna walked in, carrying market bags. Madhur, sensing the awkwardness, said, "Don't worry—after the India trip, everything will be all right."

That, of course, raised more questions.

"What's not all right?" Sapna asked, glancing at me.

"Jaideep's got ... a situation." Priyanka replied.

I quickly jumped in. "It's not a problem, more like ... confusion. I'm trying to figure out how to handle it."

"What's confusing you?" Sapna asked, unloading her groceries.

My mind quickly jumped to a plausible answer. "You remember Moe, right? My store manager?"

She nodded. "Yeah, the guy who also makes videos."

"Well, he wants to make one featuring a homeless person, but no one's agreeing. So, I suggested he ask one of his friends to play the part. He liked the idea ... and now he wants me to do it."

She paused, raising an eyebrow. "Why would you say no?"

"I'm not homeless. And I can't act."

She rolled her eyes. "How do you know you can't act?"

"Because I've never tried?"

"Then try it. If you're terrible, he won't post it."

Her confidence in me made me want to ask her out again, but I held back. She'd made her opinion all too clear.

Over the next few days, living with her became a struggle. Being near someone you have feelings for doesn't dull those feelings; it amplifies them. Every glance, every minute around her convinced me how wrong it was to stay. I couldn't stop thinking about her.

At work one morning, Moe came in to relieve me after my shift. "You ready?" he asked.

"Always."

"Here's your script. We're shooting next week."

I blinked. "Wait, what? I thought you meant 'ready to go home'."

Moe laughed. "Take the script, think it over and let me know on Monday. You're too tired to think straight right now."

I thought about what she'd said. "All right. Let's do it Monday."

"You sure? You'll be tired then, too."

"Exactly. I'll be sleep-deprived, which will make me look more authentic for the part. Homeless people don't exactly radiate energy, right?"

Moe grinned. "Now you're thinking like a filmmaker."

————◦◦◇◦◦————

The next couple of days passed with me immersing myself in the script. It was wild, really. Why would anyone believe an immigrant like me would end up homeless here? Life in India wasn't perfect, but it wasn't that bad. Still, without overthinking it, I committed to the role, trying to absorb every detail of the script.

Monday morning came too soon. Moe showed up right on time, carrying a piece of cardboard with a message scribbled on it:

"I have lost HOME but not HOPE.
I lost everything and everyone.
Please help me buy some food,
As you cannot put a SHED on my HEAD."

He handed me the sign along with a white shirt smudged with dirt, a black jacket to cover it when not filming, and a pair of trousers that looked like they'd been through hell.

"Let's get this over with." I muttered, changing into the clothes. As soon as we stepped outside the store, I thought how bad an idea this was. The city was bustling—it was Monday morning, after all—so no hiding from the flood of people. But I pushed through, acting like it was no big deal.

Our first stop was the entrance to the Queen Victoria Building. Hundreds of people streamed through every minute, paying little attention to anyone but themselves. Moe told me to sit in a corner, take off the jacket, and hold up the sign while he fiddled with his phone, setting up the camera.

Hardly a minute passed before a guy dropped a coin in front of me and said, "Good on you, mate. Never lose hope."

"Uh, thanks." I stammered, caught off guard. Moe's camera caught the exchange, and I could hear him chuckling behind me.

Then a security guard approached, eyeing me suspiciously. "You can't sit here, mate."

I looked up. "Oh, hi! It's me, I work at the store—night shifts."

He squinted, then recognition dawned. "Thought it was you, but I wasn't sure. What are you doing?"

"We're making a video." I explained. "Moe here is trying to get more views by helping a 'homeless' guy."

The guard shook his head. "Oh no, no. You can't do that here."

Moe chimed in. "Why not? We're just filming a little—"

"You post this video today, and tomorrow we'll have a crowd of people coming here, hoping to get something. It'll be chaos. I don't need that in my life."

Moe frowned. "So, where can we film?"

"Try the bridge." the guard suggested. "That's where the actual homeless people hang out."

Reluctantly, we took a tram to the bridge, finally finding a quiet spot where we wouldn't attract too much official attention. As I sat down, Moe gave me some last-minute directions.

"Remember, bro, you need to look angry, not friendly. If you don't know how to look angry, pout a little and grind your teeth. That'll do the trick. Just a little acting lesson for you."

I sighed, trying to muster the right expression, knowing full well this was going to be a long day.

———◇◇◇◇◇———

Two days later, Sapna came and woke me up, saying, "Moe has posted the video." And she showed me her mobile.

"Hey guys, my name's Alexander Mohammed. Today I decided to help the community. I'm looking for someone who needs help." Moe starts as he is standing at the QVB entrance, our first place to shoot. Then the scene moves to the bridge. There is nobody around me, and I am lying down near the bridge column. He climbs the stairs and walks up to me and says, "How are you?"

"What do you want? Why are you guys filming me?" I ask, trying to look angry.

"Sorry, sir, I don't mean to offend you. I know you were sleeping. But can I please, please, help you? Somehow?"

"How do you want to help me?"

"I'd like to bring you some food or clothes."

"But I don't have any money."

"Don't worry, I can support you, sir. I can support you. Treat me like a … I can be like your brother."

"Okay, fine." I say to show that I'm easy to persuade.

"Let's go, we can get you some food." We started walking towards the city. "If you don't mind me asking, what's the reason for you being homeless?"

My main part in the script starts, "Where should I start from? I lost everything. My family, my friends, my home. I have nothing left with me right now. I am homeless. Just another homeless. Who cares? Who cares? No one cares, anyway."

He listened to my concerns and his expressions showed concern towards me. As we reached Subway, he asked me to join him to grab a bite.

"Brother, let's have some food." As I was eating a chicken schnitzel Subway, he asked, "Has anyone offered to help you before?"

"No, not really." I say. Then, pausing to follow the directions, I continue, "Some people have come to me, but they threw food at me like I was a dog or something. Or they might give me their leftover food. And then they think they've helped someone. But I still thank them because that's the reason why I'm still alive."

We leave Subway and the video continues as we head to Target, where he buys me clean clothes and says, "If you don't mind me asking, brother, did you find a job?"

"I tried to find a job." I say while I looking at myself in the mirror and admiring my new attire, then I continue, "But people prefer not to hire people like us because we are homeless. They feel that homeless people take drugs, but everybody is not the same. Not even the government will help us because we don't have secure accommodation. The only means of survival left is to ask people for money."

His facial expression shows sadness about my life, then he says, "I was going to ask you, was your whole life like this?"

"No, it wasn't, earlier." I tell him as we leave Target in my new attire. "I wish I could go back in time and enjoy my early days. I had my family, my dad, my mum, my friends, everything. I used to go to school. I used to enjoy my life. But now everything has changed."

"What happened? Can you explain what happened, please?" he asks me when we reach the barber's for me to get a haircut.

"After my parents passed away, my brother stole everything from me by forging a property document. And this led to me living on the streets. And now that's my home. On the streets." I say while the hairdresser styles my tangled hair.

"How do you feel about becoming homeless?" he asks.

"Not good. Not good at all! It's very hard living on the streets. We often stay hungry all night; sometimes, even for days at a stretch. We don't have enough money to buy food regularly. I wouldn't wish anyone to go through what I'm experiencing right now." I say, admiring my stylish new look as we pass a shop window. Then I look at him and say, "Thanks for making my day."

"My pleasure." And the video ends.

The first thing that comes to mind is, "Nobody must ever see this video." And I decide never to talk about it again.

———◦◦◦◦◦———

"Hey, brother! I almost forgot you were back today." Govind said as I walked into my first Friday night shift after returning from India.

"I messaged you this morning." I replied, setting my things down. "Told you to take it easy this week. I'll be working full shifts—I need to earn some cash. Spent way too much in India this time."

"How was the trip?"

"Great, actually. Two weddings, Amar's birthday and time with family and friends. It was a meaningful visit, you know? I reflected on what I'd left behind, but this time it was different—no emotional baggage, no fear. I really enjoyed all my time with my parents and old friends. They've been my rock during tough times, so I made sure to personally thank each of them."

"That sounds like a good trip. You bought some gifts for them on Boxing Day, right? How'd your parents react?"

"Yeah, they were pleased! I got Dad an iPhone and Mum a handbag—small tokens of appreciation. They've done so much for me. I also brought a bunch of souvenirs for Amar. It's impossible to repay their sacrifices, but it felt good to give them something back."

"You flew in this morning?"

"Yep, landed in Melbourne, crashed at home for a bit, then came straight here. I'm ready for the night."

"You'll need that energy. I've been working two weeks straight, and I'm wiped out. I need a serious break."

"Take all the time you need."

Govind smiled. "How were your parents when they saw you?"

"They were happy to see me but worried about how much I'd been spending. Everyone I met had the same advice—finish your master's before coming back. They want me to stay focused."

"And Sapna? How's she doing?"

"She's good. Seemed happy to see me back, but honestly, I don't have much time for her right now. I have to work seven nights straight, and sleep during the day. I need to save up before the second semester starts, and my work hours get cut."

"Yeah, classes start in a month. It's going to be tough getting back into study mode after four months off."

"One step at a time. What subjects are you planning to take?"

"We were waiting for you to get back so we can decide together."

"When's the deadline?"

"Applications open next week. We've got about two weeks to submit."

"Perfect! We'll sort it out then. For now, just get some sleep. Your eyes are bloodshot."

Govind chuckled and headed out, leaving me alone to tackle the night shift. I downed a Red Bull and restocked the shelves, waiting for the usual Friday night rush. But hours passed, and barely anyone came into the store. The clubs were quiet, which was strange. I thought about calling Govind to see if anything had changed.

Suddenly, a familiar voice boomed behind me. "Long time, mate! Where've you been?"

I turned to see the giant security guard, grinning as he approached.

"I was in India for two weeks." I said. "Hope you guys didn't miss me too much."

"We missed you a bit, but you missed all the action."

"What happened? Why is it so quiet tonight?"

"There were a few overdose incidents at the clubs. One of them didn't make it."

"What? Seriously?"

"Yeah. Both clubs are under investigation now. They'll stay closed until the dust settles."

"How long will that take?"

"Hopefully, just a couple of weeks. There are places with worse drug problems than here. These clubs aren't that bad."

"This store relies on those clubs. More than 60 percent of our revenue comes from them."

"Sixty percent of our trouble comes from them, too."

"Well, your trouble is our income." I sighed. "I'll check with Moe tomorrow, see what the situation is. With any luck, I'll still have a job next week."

We chatted for a bit before he left, and I spent the rest of the night watching movies on YouTube and organising stock. As dawn approached, Moe confirmed the bad news—the clubs would be closed for at least three more weeks.

———∞◇◇∞———

In the days following my return from India, I noticed a big shift in the way Sapna treated me. She wanted to see me every day. She wanted to know more about me and my life. My life turned upside down.

I couldn't get more than four hours of sleep at a time, juggling work and spending time with her. Life felt amazing. I thought I could hear violin music all day long, not only because I'd got what I wanted but also because I was sleep-deprived. I wanted to spend time with her during the day but had to work all night, so I couldn't find time for sleep.

By the end of two weeks, I hadn't lost my job, but I'd lost all my energy. The clubs were set to reopen in three weeks and exhaustion was hitting hard.

———∞◇◇∞———

One weekday, Sarthak called. "Where are you? We're all at Govind's place, finalising subjects for next semester."

"I'm getting ready now. Be there in 15 minutes."

I rushed to get dressed and glanced out the window. It was a warm, sunny day, so I threw on a shirt and shorts. I left my apartment and took the elevator. When I got outside, though, the weather had turned freezing cold and windy. I hurried back inside to grab a jumper and pants. By the time I came back out, it had started raining. Back inside again, I grabbed an umbrella. And wouldn't you know it? As soon as I stepped out, the sun was shining again.

After all that, I finally made it to Govind's place, and we sorted out our subjects for the next semester.

---◇◇◇◇◇◇---

One quiet night, with the clubs still shut and the store unusually calm, I was sipping on a Red Bull when a man walked in.

"Good evening, mate." he said, flashing an identification card for a split second. I couldn't make out the details, but I didn't want to seem rude. "Routine safety inspection."

I'd never dealt with a safety inspection before, though I'd heard Moe talk about them. The man's calm, authoritative demeanour made me assume this was standard procedure.

"All right." I said, trying to stay composed. "What do you need to check?"

He smiled, but it was a thin smile, not reaching his eyes. "Just making sure everything's up to code. You know how it is."

I nodded, watching as he moved around the store, jotting notes on a clipboard. He checked the fire extinguisher, scanned the refrigerated section's temperature, all routine stuff. But something was off about the way he moved—too casually, like he was rehearsing rather than inspecting. Despite the odd feeling creeping up, I didn't want to cause a scene, especially on a quiet night.

After about 15 minutes, he returned to the counter. "Looks good here." he said, still scribbling. "I just need to check the back room and the cash register logs to wrap this up."

I hesitated. "The back room's off-limits to anyone but staff."

His smile tightened. "Standard procedure, mate. Gotta make sure there's nothing hazardous back there. Won't take long."

"I should call my manager, just to confirm."

"Go ahead."

I dialled Moe's number. No answer. Tried Sam—same result. They were probably asleep, as it was the middle of the night. After several failed attempts, I felt a rising sense of unease but didn't want to escalate things. Reluctantly, I led him to the back room.

It was a small, cluttered space with boxes, cleaning supplies and a live feed from the CCTV. The man scanned the room, pretending to inspect things. My instincts were screaming at me by this point, but I stood by the door, keeping my distance.

"All right." he said, glancing around. "Looks good. Now for the register logs."

I led him back to the front of the store, my heart racing. As I approached the counter, I felt him shift behind me. Suddenly, I felt cold pressure against my back—a gun.

"Don't make this difficult." he whispered, his tone now devoid of friendliness. "Open the register and the safe. Now."

My heart pounded in my chest, and I knew there was no point in resisting. A few hundred dollars wasn't worth risking my life. With trembling hands, I opened the register, the beep sounding unusually loud in the silence. He quickly stuffed the cash into a plastic bag, his movements sharp and efficient.

"Now the safe." he demanded, pushing the gun harder into my back.

"We don't have a safe here." I managed, my voice barely a whisper.

"Where's the rest of the cash, then?"

"We deposit it at the bank next door every morning."

For a moment, he stayed silent, as if weighing whether to believe me. Then he stepped back.

"All right, you've been cooperative. I'm leaving now. Don't try anything stupid, and you won't get hurt."

I stood frozen as he backed towards the door, keeping the gun trained on me. The bell above the door chimed as he slipped out. This time it carried a heavy finality.

For a short while, I was paralysed, adrenaline still coursing through my veins. When I finally regained my composure, I rushed to lock the door and immediately call the police, my hands trembling as I recounted the events.

The police arrived quickly, but the man was long gone. They took my statement, assuring me they'd do everything they could to catch him. But as the night wore on and the store's familiar neon lights flickered above me, the reality of what had happened sunk in. I felt violated—outsmarted and outmanoeuvred by a man who knew exactly what he was doing.

That night left a mark on me. For weeks afterward, I couldn't shake the image of his cold, calculating eyes or the feel of the gun pressing into my back. The convenience store, once just a place of work, had become a reminder of how close I'd come to something far worse.

When the second semester finally began, university, studies, friends and Sapna helped distract me from the robbery by walks on the beach, watching movies, cooking and having fun fights together. My vacation to India and being away from her showed her that I mean as much to her as much as she means to me. But every time at the start of my shift, that gnawing fear crept back. The store was never the same after that. Every night, I worked with a knot of anxiety, always half-expecting someone with bad intentions to walk in.

One night, as I arrived at the store to start my shift, Moe was waiting for me at the door.

"I've got some news, brother." he said, his face serious.

"Good or bad?" I asked, though his tone had already given me the answer.

"Definitely not good. The authorities have shut down both clubs. They're not reopening any time soon. There's a full-scale investigation underway, and it's going to take almost a year to resolve these cases."

"What happened?"

"They were running an underground operation—manufacturing Ecstasy and MDMA. It's the biggest drug bust Australia's seen in years."

"How do you know?"

"I don't." He paused, then added softly, "Just speculating. We'll never know." I stood there, stunned. "What does that mean for the store?"

"Sam sold it to some Turkish guy. The new management takes over in four weeks. They're doing the handover and other formalities in the meantime. But Sam told me this morning that the new owners have decided to close the store on weekend nights. They're cutting down shifts."

My stomach sank. "That's bad news for me."

Moe sighed. "Yeah, brother, I know. I'd offer you my shifts, but I need the money for my studies. It's tough for everyone right now."

I nodded. "It's fine. I'll work until the last day, but I need to start looking for another job immediately. Let me know if you hear about any openings."

"I will, for sure." he said, sticking around for a few minutes longer, offering what sympathy he could. I appreciated the gesture, but once he left, the reality hit me hard.

I sat down, going over my finances, and it dawned on me just how much I had spent lately—especially on Sapna. She wasn't committed to me, not like I'd hoped, and now I had almost no savings. I couldn't ask my family for money; that wasn't an option. I had to figure this out on my own.

I sent out a quick message to everyone I knew in Melbourne, letting them know I'd lost my job and asking if they knew of any openings. Most people responded with kind words and sympathy, but no one had a solid lead.

I stared at my phone, waiting for the message I desperately needed, but it didn't come.

Two weeks later I got a call from a friend to tell me about an opening at Grill'd in Southbank. I called the store manager. She asked me to visit the store in person for them to see my work and then decide. After a short introduction, I made up some experience in similar job profile to tilt the scales in my favour. After I finished my story, we decided Tuesday morning was the best day to showcase my extraordinary talent.

The sun was shining brightly that day, the kind of weather that makes you believe that anything is possible. I remember feeling a mix of nervous excitement and determination as I walked into Grill'd and said to a staff member, "I am here for my training shift". This is the first step towards securing a job that I thought would be my ticket to some cash and decent work experience.

As soon as I'd said this to the staff member, I was greeted by the scent of sizzling patties and fresh ingredients, a sensory overload that made my stomach grumble. The manager, a tall woman named Mary with a tattoo sleeve running up her arm, gave me a quick nod and handed me a black apron with the Grill'd logo emblazoned on it.

"Ready to get started?" Her grin was equal parts welcoming and challenging.

I nodded, trying to mask my nerves with a smile. "Absolutely."

The first hour was a blur. Mary gave me a quick tour of the kitchen, introducing me to the team. Everyone seemed friendly enough, but I couldn't shake the feeling that I was the odd one out. The kitchen was a well-oiled machine, each person playing a crucial role in delivering the perfect burger. There was Judith, the grill master who flipped patties with the kind of finesse that only comes from years of practice, and Declan, who handled the fryer like an artist with a paintbrush.

My role was simple, or so it seemed. I was to assist with food preparation and keep the kitchen spotless. Easy enough, right? *Wrong.*

The first task was slicing vegetables. Mary handed me a sharp knife and pointed to a mountain of tomatoes, lettuce and onions that needed to be prepped for the lunch rush. "Just keep your fingers out of the way, and you'll be fine." she said, half-joking.

I've been chopping vegetables every day for the past seven months, but now, doing it under pressure, with a clock ticking and the knowledge that these slices would end up on someone's plate, was a whole different game. My hands trembled as I tried to keep up with the pace set by the others. Before long, I'd sliced my first tomato. It was uneven, with jagged edges that looked more like the work of a toddler than a potential employee.

Mary glanced over and frowned. "Try to keep them uniform. Consistency is key here."

I nodded and tried again, but the pressure was getting to me. My confidence was already wavering. My slices were either too thick or too thin, and I could feel Mary's eyes on me, silently judging every cut. It wasn't long before I'd cut my finger—a small nick, but enough to draw blood. Embarrassed, I grabbed a Band-aid and tried to shake it off, but the damage was done.

Next up was the grill, where things really started to go downhill. Judith handed me a spatula and showed me how to flip the patties, explaining the importance of timing. "You've got to get it just right." she said. "Too long, and it's overcooked and burnt. Too short, and it's raw."

Simple enough in theory, but in practice, it was a nightmare for me. The patties seemed to have a mind of their own, refusing to flip when I wanted them to. I struggled to keep track of which ones were ready to flip and which ones needed more time. In the chaos, I managed to burn a few, turning what should have been perfectly cooked burgers into charred, inedible lumps.

Mary was there in an instant, her expression a mix of frustration and concern. "It's okay, it happens." she said, but I could tell she wasn't impressed.

By the time the lunchtime rush hit, I was in full panic mode. The kitchen was a whirlwind of activity, orders flying in faster than we could fill them. I tried to keep up, but it was like trying to swim against a riptide. My movements were clumsy, my timing off and I could feel myself becoming a burden to the team rather than an asset.

Then came the final straw. A large order came in, and in my haste to help out, I accidentally dropped a tray of freshly grilled patties onto the floor. The entire kitchen went silent as the reality of what had just happened sank in. Mary looked at me, and I could see the disappointment in her eyes. "That's a lot of wasted food." she said quietly.

I scrambled to clean up the mess, but the damage was done. I felt like I'd failed, not just at the task, but at everything I'd set out to achieve. The rest of the shift passed in a blur, with me trying to stay out of the way as much as possible.

When the shift finally ended, Mary called me into her office. I knew what was coming, but that didn't make it any easier to hear.

"Jaideep, I can see you're trying, but this job might not be the best fit for you." she said, her tone gentle but firm. "It's a fast-paced environment, and I'm not sure it's where your strengths lie."

I nodded, feeling a mix of relief and disappointment. She was right—I wasn't cut out for the high-pressure world of a busy kitchen. As much as I wanted a job to keep myself running, I just didn't have the right skills. We shook hands and I left the restaurant, my mind swirling with thoughts of what I could have done differently.

As I walked back home, I felt a failure. But as the initial sting faded, I knew that this wasn't the end of the world. Not every opportunity is the right fit, and sometimes, failure is just a door to something better. I might not have got the job, but I walked away with a valuable lesson in humility and self-awareness. As if the weather was reflecting this, it was winter, and the chilly Melbourne winds had a way of cutting right through you.

One evening of those frustrating days, I was sitting on a bench in Federation Square, watching the world go by, when my phone buzzed with a message from Rohit, my dear friend and confidant, someone who always seemed to have his finger on the pulse of the city. The message was short but full of promise: "Mate, I've got something that might help you out. Meet me at Flinders Street at 8." When I met Rohit later that day, he had that familiar spark in his eye. That usually meant he was onto something good. "Jaideep." he said with a grin, "have you heard about Uber Eats? It's just starting here, and they're paying crazy money for deliveries. You won't believe it—they're offering $23 an hour, and all you have to do is deliver one order per hour during lunch and dinner. Easy money, mate."

"I'm intrigued." The idea of earning that much with minimal effort was tempting, especially when I was struggling to make ends meet. "Uber Eats is just launching in Australia, and it's offering lucrative rates to attract delivery partners. There's no minimum order fee for customers, which means that most of the deliveries will be nearby, usually within a few blocks." Rohit told me.

"It sounds too good to be true. But there's was one hitch: I don't have a bike."

"That's where Sapna comes in." Rohit said with a knowing smile, referring to my St Kilda bike ride. Even though we were living together I hadn't spoken to her in a while because of me not being in right place and she being busy with her uni, too, but when I reached out to explain my situation, she didn't hesitate. "Take it, Jaideep. You need it more than I do right now."

With the bicycle in hand, I signed up for Uber Eats, ready to hit the streets and to start this new chapter.

The first few days were exhilarating. Melbourne's CBD is a maze of narrow lanes, towering buildings and hidden alleyways, each one leading to a new adventure. The orders were frequent but manageable, often just a few blocks away. The weather was on my side, too, with clear skies and a gentle breeze making the rides almost enjoyable. It felt good to be moving, to be doing something productive. The work was simple enough—pick up food from the restaurant, navigate through the city streets, and deliver it to the customer. The $23 per hour was more than enough to cover my expenses, and for the first time in a long while, I felt a sense of relief.

However, the honeymoon period didn't last long. Melbourne's CBD, with its seemingly charming cobblestoned streets and hilly terrain, soon revealed its true colours. Riding a bicycle through those streets was anything but easy. The city's unpredictable weather also began to play tricks on me. On one occasion, I found myself pedalling furiously through a downpour, the rain soaking me to the skin and making the roads slick and dangerous. The once-pleasant breeze turned into a harsh wind that seemed determined to push me backwards, making every delivery a battle against the elements.

To add to the challenge, I found I wasn't the only one who'd jumped on the Uber Eats bandwagon. Word had spread fast, and soon, Melbourne's streets were flooded with new delivery drivers, many of them international students like me. These newcomers were well-prepared, armed with electric bikes that made my old bicycle look like an ancient relic. The electric bikes zipped through the streets with ease, while I struggled to keep up, panting and sweating as I tried to make my deliveries on time.

The increasing competition brought with it a new set of challenges. Uber Eats, noticing the surge in drivers, decided to change the pay structure. Instead of the guaranteed $AU23 per hour, now, I had to complete at least one delivery each hour for three consecutive hours to earn the hourly rate. If I failed to meet this target, I'd be paid based on the delivery rates, which were around $5 per trip.

This change hit hard. The once-reliable income became irregular and unpredictable. Some days, I was able to meet the target and earn the hourly rate, but on other days, especially when the orders were sparse or too far apart, I found myself struggling to complete even one delivery in an hour. At times, after hours of pedalling through the city, I'd return home with just $10 more in my account. The joy I initially felt began to fade, replaced by frustration and a sense of hopelessness.

The final blow came about a month after I'd started. By then, Uber Eats had grown exponentially. The service had become incredibly popular, with more and more drivers joining every day. In response, Uber Eats made yet another change to the pay structure, eliminating the hourly rate altogether. From that point on, we were paid based on the number of deliveries we completed only.

This shift turned the once-enjoyable job into a race against time. I found myself competing not only with the terrain and weather but also with hundreds of other drivers, all vying for the same orders. The pressure was immense and the earnings became even more erratic. Some days, I could make a decent amount if the orders were steady, but on others, I barely made enough to cover my expenses.

Struggling to make ends meet as an Uber Eats delivery driver in Melbourne was not how I envisioned my life while pursuing a master's degree. The pay structure, designed to favour peak hours, clashed directly with my evening lectures. Those hours from 6 to 9 p.m., when most people were enjoying dinner or unwinding after a day's work, were the most crucial for me to attend classes. I had invested a significant amount in my education, and missing lectures was not an option. Yet, the necessity of earning a living forced me into a relentless cycle of stress, where I was torn between academic commitments and the need to keep my finances afloat.

One such evening, as I rushed through the city delivering meals, the weight of my circumstances pressing heavily on my shoulders, I received a call from Rohit. His message gave me a glimmer of hope I hadn't felt in weeks.

"Jaideep, there's a job opening at the car wash at Melbourne Airport Europcar." he said, his tone filled with encouragement. "My friend found out about it. They need someone immediately."

I didn't hesitate. Despite the gruelling experience of cycling through Melbourne's CBD for Uber Eats and the disappointing returns it brought, this opportunity at the car wash seemed like a chance for stability—something I desperately needed.

The next day, I arrived at the Melbourne Airport Europcar, my nerves tingling with anticipation and apprehension. The manager, a no-nonsense Asian man, briefed me on the job. "You'll start on the vacuum cleaner line." he said. "It's the first task for every newcomer."

Vacuuming cars was far more taxing than I imagined. My first day was a blur of noise, sweat and sheer exhaustion. The vacuum cleaner was heavier than it looked, and I had just 45 seconds to vacuum one side of a car while my partner tackled the other side. The work was relentless, requiring not just speed but precision, and it left me drained.

At the end of the day, the manager handed me an employment form and requested my bank account details. This small, practical gesture confirmed my new reality—I was now a car-wash attendant.

As the days turned into weeks, the physical demands of the job began to take a toll on me. My arms ached from wielding the vacuum cleaner, my back protested from the constant bending and stretching, and my spirit sagged under the weight of repetitive labour. The job was more than just physically demanding; it was a blow to my pride. I had never even washed my father's car back home, considering it beneath me. Now, I was washing other people's cars for money. The irony wasn't lost on me.

But I swallowed my pride. The necessity of survival had a way of humbling even the most stubborn of egos. I told myself this was temporary, a means to an end, and I kept going.

The first month was the hardest. Every day felt like a marathon, and I found myself longing for the simpler tasks at the car wash—those that didn't involve the heavy vacuum cleaner. I observed my colleagues, hoping that after putting in my time on the vacuum line, I might be assigned to something less strenuous. Outside cleaning, perhaps, or the task of driving cars back and forth between the airport and the wash station—anything that didn't involve lugging around that cumbersome machine.

By the time the second month rolled around, I was still stuck on the vacuum cleaner line. My body had adapted somewhat to the physical demands, but the work remained gruelling. I watched as others were rotated to different tasks, hoping each day that my turn would come. Yet, despite my growing proficiency, I was still tethered to the vacuum.

As the third month began, my energy and motivation were at an all-time low. The optimism I had clung to when I first took the job had faded, replaced by a desperate longing for change. I wasn't made for this—I wasn't built to lift heavy equipment day in and day out. My body wasn't giving up on me, but it was sending signals that this wasn't sustainable. The work wasn't just exhausting; it was demoralising. I found myself dreading each new day, wondering how much longer I could keep this up.

The most difficult part was reconciling this job with the aspirations I had when I first came to Melbourne. I was supposed to be a student, focusing on lectures, assignments and exams—not spending my days at a car wash and my nights too tired to study. I'd come to Melbourne with dreams of building a a life outside my comfort zone, and now those dreams felt like they were slipping away, buried under the relentless demands of my current reality.

But despite the hardships, I knew I couldn't quit. I had to keep going, at least until I found something else—something that would allow me to balance work with my studies, something that didn't drain me of the energy I needed to pursue my education. I had sacrificed too much to be here, and I couldn't let it all go to waste.

Every day at the car wash was a test of endurance, both physical and mental. I pushed through, motivated by the belief that this struggle was temporary, that I was building resilience for the future. Each car I vacuumed, each long day I completed, was a step closer to something better, even if I couldn't yet see what that would be.

In those moments of doubt, I reminded myself of the bigger picture—the degree I was working towards, the opportunities that lay ahead once I completed my studies. This job, as harsh as it was, was a bridge to a future where I wouldn't have to choose between making a living and pursuing my dreams.

As the third month ended, I found myself at a crossroads. I knew I had to find a way out, a job that was more in line with my abilities and aspirations.

One morning, I reached Europcar early. The manager caught me as soon as I got off the bus and asked, "How did your three months go?"

"They went well."

"Be truthful, mate. It's fine if you don't like it as well. Nobody likes this job anyway."

"The journey is humbling, yes, but it's also taught me resilience and the value of hard work. It reminded me that no job is beneath me, and that sometimes, the path to success is paved with challenges that test our limits and shape our character. I'm being tested, and though I feel close to breaking, I know I'll come out of this experience stronger, more determined, and ready for whatever comes next."

"Where do you stay?"

"In the city currently. My lease is about to expire in one month. So, I am looking for a place somewhere in city."

"Have you found another place yet?"

After he asked me this question, I shared the details of the stunning apartment I'd inspected in Southbank last week. "You wouldn't believe the view from this place." I began, pulling out my phone to show him the photo I had taken.

"The apartment itself is a spacious three-bedroom unit, modern and sleek, with floor-to-ceiling windows that perfectly frame the Melbourne skyline. This is what you'd see every day." I said, passing him the phone with the image. He studied it, taking in the scene.

"This is from the apartment?" he asked, impressed. I nodded enthusiastically.

"Yes, it's right from the living room. The building is high up, so you get this unobstructed view of the entire city. That's Eureka Tower over there on the right—it's so close that it feels like you could almost reach out and touch it." The tower's gold crown was glinting, catching the last rays of daylight, while the city lights started to twinkle.

"The entire skyline lights up at night." I continued. "It's incredible. You can see the Crown Casino down there too, with all its neon signs lighting up Southbank. I could just imagine sitting in the living room or on the balcony, watching the city come alive as the sun sets. It's like a living painting, changing every hour."

My manager smiled, clearly picturing it. "Looks like a dream. How was the rest of the apartment?"

"The apartment itself is as amazing as the view." I said. "Three bedrooms, all of them with big windows that flood the rooms with light. The master bedroom even has a view of the skyline, which I think would be incredible to wake up to every morning. The kitchen is modern, with all the latest appliances, and it opens out into the living room, so you're never far from that view." I added, "it's right in Southbank, close to everything—restaurants, cafes, the arts district. It's perfect for getting into the city or just enjoying what the area has to offer."

He looked back at the photo, nodding appreciatively. "That sounds like a great find. I can see why you're excited about it. It's not just the apartment, but the whole lifestyle it offers."

"Exactly." I said, feeling a sense of anticipation as I thought about the possibility of living there. "I can already see myself enjoying that view every day."

"That's good! Because we have an opening nearby at Richmond Europcar. It would be easier for you to get there. Also, only few cars come over there each day. So, it's an easier job. Pay's the same, but travel costs and time and the workload would be lower, too." he said.

I moved into the new place and enjoyed time with my roommates. With my new job I could manage my studies well. It was easy money; hardly anything to do. Work would start at 8 a.m. and finish at 12 p.m. In four hours, I only had to clean a few cars. The pay was very low, but enough. This move distanced me from Sapna for good.

My second semester finished with struggles in my personal life, also financially and emotionally. I'd scored a HD with a 3.8 GPA in my first semester, but in my second semester I just passed with a 2.3 GPA—a drastic drop. I was desperate to get a job which would pay better in the semester break.

During this break I could again work for 40 hours per week and I had time to look for better-paying jobs. In the free time at the carwash I would apply for jobs on various apps.

One afternoon, while taking time off from my tense life and chilling with my roommate Rigved, I got a text. "Join our team in an exciting opportunity to contribute to important medical research! We are seeking participants for a nicotine study. Earn while helping advance scientific knowledge. Must be 18-65, healthy, and willing to comply with study requirements. Compensation provided. Apply now to make a difference!"

I showed that message to Rigved. After reading that message, he asked, "How much are they paying?"

After back and forth on a few messages I replied, "It is a 28-day test. For all 28 days I will have to stay in their premises. Food and accommodation included. I can select the cuisine, too. I will be under their supervision so that they can see me if I am not smoking."

"How much are they paying?"

"Twelve thousand dollars."

"That's an insane amount of money. But do you want to do that? This is a test; they don't know what will happen. There must be side-effects too that they're not yet aware of. It's dangerous. Think about it. Nobody gives out easy money."

"I know, but I'm desperate for money. Just one month could solve my problem for next semester."

The offer was tempting—$12,000 for 28 days, all expenses covered. I couldn't stop thinking about the money. With the kind of financial pressure I was under, it felt like a godsend. Accommodation and food included. All I had to do was participate in a nicotine-testing program at The Alfred hospital.

The risks were there, of course, but $12,000 in just under a month? That kind of money could help me in ways nothing else could. I met the criteria without trying. The thought of earning that amount of money for a month's commitment was incredibly appealing, especially considering my dwindling bank balance and mounting bills.

But beneath the surface, a nagging doubt began to fester. Nicotine testing wasn't just some casual survey or observational study. It was an experiment on my body, my health. The risks were substantial, and I couldn't ignore the potential long-term consequences. Would I end up damaging my health permanently for a quick financial fix? The thought gnawed at me, but every time I considered backing out, the dollar signs flashed before my eyes, urging me to push those concerns aside.

As the day approached, my anxiety only grew. I kept trying to rationalise it—plenty of people smoke for years and manage to live long lives, right? Surely, a controlled environment at a hospital wouldn't be so bad. I convinced myself that the money was worth the risk, that I was just overthinking it.

But when I arrived at The Alfred hospital, that sense of unease only grew stronger. I wasn't just making some decision in the abstract anymore; this was happening, and it was happening to me. I took a deep breath and tried to calm the storm in my head. Inside, it was cool, the sterile smell of the hospital filling my senses as I walked to the registration desk. My name was already on the list.

As I waited for my turn, I glanced around at the others. A few looked calm, others as anxious as I felt. My thoughts were interrupted by a buzzing in my pocket. It was a text message from an unknown number. I frowned, unlocking my phone to read it.

"Hi, Jaideep. We're offering $AU700 per day for a two-hour job. Interested? Get back to us ASAP."

I blinked, reading the message again. My first instinct was to dismiss it as a scam. The timing was suspicious, almost as if the universe was playing a cruel joke on me. Who offers $700 for two hours of work? But the idea of making that much in a day—without the health risks—planted itself in my mind. Even if it was a scam, it seemed safer than what I was about to do. What if this was my way out? What if this was the universe telling me not to go through with the testing?

Another message popped up.

"We are an independent finance company. Call us if interested."

The doubt about nicotine testing that had been nagging at me all morning suddenly became overwhelming. I glanced towards the entrance, the way I came in, then back at the elevator that would take me to the testing area. Could I really walk away from $12,000, just like that? But could I also gamble with my health, my future? The decision weighed heavily on my shoulders.

Finally, I stood up, grabbed my things and walked out of the hospital without looking back. The fresh air hit my face as I stepped outside, and I felt a rush of relief, tinged with anxiety about what I'd just done. The fear of missing out on the $12,000 was still there, but it was now outweighed by the overwhelming sense that I'd made the right call.

The phone rang just as I stepped out of the hospital, still reeling from my decision to walk away from the nicotine-testing program. My head was a jumble of doubts and second guesses, but the caller ID showing an unknown number caught my attention. I knew it was them—the independent finance company offering that suspiciously lucrative job.

"Hello?" I answered, my voice betraying a mix of curiosity and wariness.

"Hi, Jaideep." a smooth voice replied. "This is James from Global Transfer Solutions. We spoke earlier about the job opportunity."

I nodded, even though he couldn't see me, trying to steady my nerves. "Yeah, you said something about $700 a day for a two-hour job. That sounds too good to be true."

"I understand your concern." James said, his tone friendly and reassuring. "But let me explain how it works. We're a backend support service for several financial institutions. Our main role is to facilitate overseas money transfers. Sometimes, due to regulatory restrictions and transaction limits, we need to route funds through individual accounts to speed up the process."

"Okay .." I was still unconvinced. "So, what exactly would I be doing?"

"Here's the deal." he began. "We will transfer a certain amount of money into your bank account every day. Your job is to withdraw that cash and then transfer it to several different accounts, according to the instructions we'll provide. It's a straightforward process, and for this, we compensate you with more than $700 per day."

My mind was racing. The words sounded professional, even logical—but something about it still felt off.

"And this is legal?" I asked, needing to hear it directly.

"Absolutely!" James replied without hesitation. "We work with reputable financial institutions, and everything is above-board. You're just helping facilitate the transfer of funds—think of it as an extension of what banks do daily. We've had numerous people like you working with us, and there's never been any issue."

I was quiet, digesting his words. I wasn't naïve. I'd heard stories of money-laundering schemes and knew how easy it was to get caught up in something illegal. But $700 a day? That kind of money could change everything for me. This seemed like an answer to my prayers.

"Listen, I get that you're hesitant." James continued, picking up on my silence. "But to put your mind at ease, we'll provide you with a written agreement outlining everything. You'll have it in black and white that this is a job with the company."

The offer was tempting, dangerously so. I still felt, deep down, that this was shady, probably illegal, but my circumstances left me with little room to be picky. Besides, with the written agreement, I'd have something to fall back on if things went south.

"Okay." I finally said. "I'm in. Send me the agreement, and I'll get started."

"Excellent choice, Jaideep." James replied, a hint of triumph in his voice. "I'll send over the details and agreement right away. Once you've reviewed and signed, we'll begin the transfers tomorrow. But before beginning the transfer we will need your passport copy and residential proof to enter in our system."

As I hung up the phone, I couldn't shake the unease gnawing at the back of my mind, but I pushed those thoughts aside. The written agreement would protect me—or so I convinced myself.

That night, I lay awake in bed, staring at the ceiling, questioning everything. The first $7,000 hit my account early in the next morning, just as James had promised. Seeing that amount in my balance was both thrilling and terrifying. The money was real, but the unease I'd felt since agreeing to this job hadn't subsided. My phone buzzed, snapping me out of my thoughts. A message from James detailed the next steps.

"Withdraw the $7,000 in cash. Use different branches, no more than $2,000 from each. Then, transfer the money using Western Union and MoneyGram to the accounts provided below. Remember, for MoneyGram, use different 7-Eleven locations."

I stared at the screen, the weight of what I was about to do sinking in. This wasn't just a simple task; this was money laundering, plain and simple. My hands felt clammy as I read through the instructions again, each word solidifying the illegality of the job. But what could I do? I was already in too deep. The instant that money hit my account, I became complicit. I had to follow through. No turning back now.

With a heavy heart and a knot in my stomach, I set out to complete the tasks. The first stop was a local branch where I withdrew the initial $2,000. The teller gave me a polite smile as she handed me the cash, oblivious to the moral turmoil raging inside me. I forced a return smile, pocketing the money before moving on to the next location.

The transactions at Western Union were straightforward but felt wrong in every possible way. The first two went smoothly, and I moved on to the 7-Elevens for the MoneyGram transfers. Each time I walked into a store, my heart pounded, expecting someone to question why I was sending large sums of money to strangers overseas. But no one did. The transactions went through without a hitch, and by the end of the day, I had transferred $6,000 to accounts scattered across the globe.

That left me with $1,000 still in my possession. I waited for James to send more instructions, but nothing came. As the hours ticked by, I grew more anxious. Was something wrong? Had I missed a message? Finally, unable to bear the uncertainty any longer, I called James.

"Hey, James, it's Jaideep." I said, trying to keep my voice steady. "I've completed the transfers for today, but I still have $1,000 left. Should I wait for further instructions?"

There was a brief pause on the other end before James replied, "No need to worry about that. The remaining $1,000 is your pay for today. Just hold onto it."

Relief washed over me, but it was quickly followed by a deeper sense of dread. I was now holding onto dirty money. The reality of what I was doing was undeniable, but so was the cash in my hands. I told myself that I needed this money, that I didn't have any other options. But each time I tried to justify my actions, the knot in my stomach tightened.

This process repeated itself every day for the next week. Each morning, $7,000 would arrive in my account, and each day, I would withdraw the cash from different branches, doing my best to stay under the radar. By now, I had perfected the routine:

withdraw, transfer, repeat. The tellers at the bank began to recognise me, though they never asked questions, just smiled politely as they handed over the money. I would then make my rounds to the 7-Elevens, sending off the cash through MoneyGram as instructed.

The sheer volume of money passing through my hands was staggering. Each time I completed the transactions, I would receive a message from James confirming that everything was in order, followed by the reassurance that the remaining $1,000 was mine to keep. As the week progressed, I began to numb myself to the guilt.

By the end of the week, I'd handled nearly $50,000. I should have felt proud—or at least relieved—that everything had gone smoothly, but instead, I felt trapped. Every day, the weight of what I was doing pressed down harder, but I kept going. I convinced myself that as long as I followed the instructions to the letter, I'd be fine. But deep down, I knew there was no safe way out of this.

The money was good—better than anything I'd ever earned—but it came with a price. I was playing a dangerous game, one where the rules were constantly shifting, and the stakes were higher than I was willing to admit. I had the cash, but I'd lost something far more valuable: my peace of mind. The weight of that grew heavier with each passing day, but as much as I wanted to stop, I couldn't. I was in too deep. No turning back now.

Next evening, as the sun dipped below the horizon, I leaned back in my chair, feeling the exhaustion of the day finally catch up with me. Rigved, my friend and confidant, sat across from me, a knowing smile on his face.

"How was your Saturday?" he asked, breaking the comfortable silence.

I sighed, a mix of relief and contentment washing over me. "It was good. You know, Saturday is my time to relax. No transactions from James today, thank God. I made $5,000 over the week. I deposited $4,000 in my account and kept $1,000 in cash, just in case."

Rigved nodded, understanding the delicate balance I was trying to maintain. "That's good, man. You need some downtime."

"I do." I agreed. "Had cricket umpiring today. Three games. It was exactly what I needed—just to focus on the game, nothing else. Cricket always helps me calm my nerves."

"How were the matches?" he asked.

"They were great. Standing out there for hours, it's like all the stress just melts away. I felt like myself again, not caught up in all the craziness."

Rigved smiled, seeing the change in my demeanour. "Sounds like you had a good day. After all that, you'll probably sleep like a baby tonight."

I chuckled, nodding. "Yeah, I think I will. It's funny—after everything that's been going on, just standing out there in the middle of the field made me feel at peace. Tonight, I'm going to bed without a worry."

And for the first time in a while, I believed it.

The weekend passed in a blur of mundane activities—catching up on sleep, a bit of cricket, and trying to forget the stress of the past week. But Monday morning brought reality crashing back. I woke up early, as usual, and grabbed my phone to check my bank account, eager to see the $7,000 I was expecting. But instead of the usual notification, I was greeted with a message that made my heart stop.

"Your account has been locked due to suspicious transactions. Please visit your nearest branch for assistance."

Panic set in. I sat there, staring at the screen, my mind racing. What had gone wrong? Was it over? Had they found out? My thoughts spiralled as I tried to think of what to do next. The first thing that came to mind was the $1,000 in cash I had on hand from the last transaction. If things went south, I needed a cover story.

I quickly got dressed and went to find Rigved, still half-asleep in his room. "Hey, Rigved." I said, trying to keep my voice steady. "I need you to hold onto this for me." I handed him the cash. "If anyone asks, just say I was repaying you a loan, okay?"

Rigved looked confused but nodded. "Sure, man. What's going on?"

"I'm not sure yet." With that, I headed out the door, my stomach churning with fear. The short walk to the bank felt like an eternity. My mind was filled with worst-case scenarios: the police waiting for me, my account being permanently frozen, or worse, being implicated in a crime far larger than I could handle. When I arrived at the branch, the atmosphere inside felt different—more tense than usual. I approached the front desk, trying to look as normal as possible, but my nerves were getting the better of me. "I received a notification that my account has been locked." I told the teller, my voice barely above a whisper. She glanced at her screen and then looked at me with a mix of concern and suspicion.

"Please wait here. The manager will see you shortly."

The minutes ticked by as I sat in the waiting area, the anxiety building with every second. Finally, the manager, a stern-looking man in his late forties, appeared and motioned for me to follow him to his office.

Once inside, he closed the door and gestured for me to sit. He took a seat behind his desk, folding his hands together as he directed a piercing gaze at me.

"How much money are you expecting to see in your account this morning?" he asked, his tone neutral but laced with an underlying tension.

"Uh, $7,000." I replied, my voice trembling.

The manager's expression didn't change. "Son, your account has $60,000 in it right now."

Sixty thousand? I felt the blood drain from my face. That wasn't part of the plan. I could barely process what he was saying.

The manager continued, "We've been monitoring your account due to the large sums of money being deposited and withdrawn. I need to ask you some questions, and I suggest you answer them truthfully. How did you get involved in this?"

I swallowed hard. No point in lying. "A man named James contacted me." I began, explaining the process of how I would receive money, withdraw it, and transfer it using various portals. I recounted everything in detail, from the initial conversation to the instructions I received daily.

The manager listened carefully, nodding occasionally but never relaxing his stern manner. When I finished, he leaned back in his chair and sighed.

"This is serious, Jaideep. The police might be interested in this case, but as of now, it's just a financial matter. Thankfully, we caught it before it became something much bigger. But you need to understand what you were doing is illegal."

I nodded, feeling a mix of shame and relief.

"I didn't mean to get involved in anything illegal. I just … I needed the money desperately. I didn't know what else to do."

The manager's expression softened slightly, but he remained firm. "Desperation can make us do things we wouldn't normally consider, but you're an educated man. What did you study?"

"I have a bachelor's in electrical engineering." I croaked. "And I'm currently studying for a master's in engineering management."

The manager raised an eyebrow, clearly surprised. "You've studied this much, and yet you didn't see the warning signs?"

"I knew it wasn't right." I admitted, my voice breaking. "But I was out of options. I needed the money to survive here. I've been struggling for so long ... "

He sighed again, this time with a hint of empathy.

"I understand the pressures you're under, but there are legal ways to earn money. This could have ended very differently for you. I'm going to have to file a report on this, but I'll note that you've been cooperative. It's up to the authorities now."

I nodded, feeling a weight lift off my shoulders, but at the same time, a new burden settled in its place. I'd narrowly escaped a disaster, but the consequences of my actions were far from over.

He asked me to sit at a desk while he filled out some forms before I left. As I sat, I felt a strange mix of emotions—relief that I wasn't in handcuffs, fear of what might come next, and a deep, gnawing regret for allowing myself to get involved in something so dangerous. The $60,000 in my account wasn't mine, and it never would be. But what mattered now was figuring out how to move forward, how to rebuild from this mess.

To kill time I called Rigved and explained everything. He listened quietly, both shocked and concerned for me.

"You really got yourself into some deep trouble, man." he said when I finished.

"I know! I just hope I can get out of it without ruining my life completely."

"You will. But you've got to be smarter from here on. No more shortcuts."

"Yeah. No more shortcuts."

"On the same note, struggling so much, doesn't it make you want to go back to India?"

"Every day man, every day! I wake up to the thought of going back to India. But then I think about the main reason for leaving India other than cricket or proving something to my dad."

"What is it?"

"I wanted to get out of my comfort zone. Life in India was too easy for me."

BEYOND THE CLOUDS
LIES CLARITY

As soon as I got out of the bank, I knew I had to take control of the situation.

I called James, keeping my voice steady despite the fear gnawing at me.

"James, I just got out of the police station." I lied, letting the words sink in. "You messed up big time by sending $60,000 in one transaction. They're all over it now. Thanks for everything you did last week, but I'm out."

Silence on the other end, then James mumbled something in a foreign language before hanging up. I knew I had to distance myself from this mess completely. He called me a couple of times, but I didn't answer, still too shaken to deal with him.

The bank had already taken action. They closed my earlier account for four days. I was waiting for their further advice. When I visited them, they told me they'd opened a new account, transferring all my money over except for the last $60K. It was a clean slate, but it came with a heavy price—both financially and emotionally.

In a week, I was back on my feet. And I'd managed to get Global Transfer Solutions off my back.

I could finally breathe a little easier, but the whole ordeal left me shaken. It was a close call, and I knew I had to tread carefully from now on. The desperation that had driven me to this point had almost destroyed everything, but I was determined to learn from it and move forward. No more shortcuts. No more risks. It was time to start over the right way.

One day I got call from Sarthak, my friend. "Hello, how are you?" he asked.

"Relaxing, looking for a good part-time job. In the last couple of months, I did some cover shifts at the store and umpiring on weekends. That money laundering helped me to take a breather for some time, but it's over now." I told him. "What's up with you? What pushed you to remember me today?"

"I'm doing good, too. Just finished my shift at Domino's. I called you today because the other place where I do casual jobs is looking for some more people. Just wanted to know if you're interested."

"Always interested, mate. What's the job?"

"It's traffic surveying. I just do whatever they ask me to do. They hire students like us to do their manual surveys."

"Nice! I'm in. Who should I contact?"

"I'll forward your contact details to them. Expect a text or call. They prefer texts because it's easy to broadcast."

"Okay. No problems, let me know if you need anything."

"Yes, now, are you prepared for the take-home test next week on Performance Management?" he asked.

"Almost, yes. Not sure what to prepare for the take-home test. Time flies so fast. Half of the third semester is already done."

"Yes. Let's see what it is next week."

After a short while I got a text saying, "Hi, this is Aaron from Traffic Australia. You were referred by Sarthak for upcoming projects. Please reply Yes if interested in working with us."

I immediately replied, "Yes."

"Thanks for confirming. Meet Jaydeep on Tuesday morning at Ampol Footscray petrol station at 5:00 a.m." They added the contact information of Jaydeep Verma.

I checked the location, and saw I need to leave home at 4:00 a.m. to reach there in time.

The first day, I got ready and reached the location exactly at 5.00 a.m. Two white Hyundai iLoads with orange paint in patches approached the petrol pump. They passed me, parked inside and went in. I followed them and I was followed by another young guy.

"I am Jaydeep. You Jaideep?" he asked jokingly.

"Yes, I am."

Then he called other young guy and a colleague of his, "This is Mihir and Smit."

I turned to both and greeted them. "Answer me a simple question." Jaydeep said to me. "Is this the first time we are meeting?" he asked.

"Yes."

"Have *you* messaged me at any time before coming here?" he asked me. I wondered why he seemed so cross.

"No, but I will message you every time going forward." I said. Mihir laughed, but Jaydeep didn't.

Then he turned to Smit. "Look, you've sent me ten messages since yesterday. One at night then one before leaving home. We have a life too, so don't send me messages at odd hours."

Then he turned to me. "We are a team from now. And do not message me before the given time unless it's very important."

"Noted, boss." And we jumped into the car. On the way, Jaydeep explained how the job would work.

"I'm the team leader." he said, glancing over at me. "I'll handle the technical aspects—installing the equipment, checking the camera footage and making sure everything's set up right."

My role was simpler but still crucial.

"Your job is to bring me the ladder, camera, box and batteries." he continued. "The ladder's heavy, so we'll share the load. I'll help out when needed, depending on the situation."

I nodded, taking it all in. Jaydeep made it clear that while he handled the tech side, we'd be working closely together. It wasn't just about strength—it was about teamwork.

The early morning chill was biting, but the promise of a full day's work ahead kept us focused. As Jaydeep drove, I was mentally preparing for what lay ahead.

Our first stop was a location nearby. We pulled up, and I heaved the heavy ladder out of the van, feeling the weight in my muscles as I carried it to the site. The ladder was cumbersome, and with the batteries weighing 1.3 kilos each, it was clear this job would test my physical limits.

Jaydeep was efficient, already setting up the equipment while I struggled with the ladder. After the first camera was installed, he turned to me with a task. "Hold this number plate and stand in front of the camera." he instructed. "We need to check if it's captured clearly."

I positioned the plate in front of the camera lens, trying to stay as still as possible. Jaydeep fiddled with the controls, his focus intense. Once he was satisfied, he called me over and showed me the footage on his monitor.

"What do you think?" he asked, inviting my novice opinion.

I glanced at the screen; the number plate was clear. "It looks good to me." I said, trying to sound confident.

Jaydeep nodded. "Great. Let's move on."

The day continued in a similar rhythm. We drove from one location to another across Melbourne CBD, each stop requiring the same process: unloading equipment, installing cameras, checking footage. My arms grew sore from carrying the ladder, and my back ached from bending and lifting. Yet, with each successful installation, I felt a growing sense of accomplishment.

Jaydeep guided me through the day, occasionally offering tips on how to handle the equipment more efficiently or how to position the cameras for optimal coverage. Despite the physical strain, his calm attitude made the work more manageable. He'd show me the footage, ask for my input and explain the part the cameras would play in the larger system they were installing.

By late afternoon, we'd installed 30 cameras, the final one at Port Melbourne. As the sun set, casting a golden glow over the water and the shipping containers, I paused, taking in the serene sight. The hustle of the CBD felt like a distant memory as I stood by the water, the gentle lapping of waves soothing my tired muscles.

Jaydeep made his final adjustments and joined me. We stood in silence, both appreciating the quiet beauty of the evening. The containers, now silhouetted against the fading light, created a stark contrast to the bustling city we'd just left behind.

"This view makes the hard work worth it, doesn't it?" Jaydeep said, breaking the silence.

I nodded, feeling a sense of peace settle over me. "Yeah, it really does."

———∞∞∞∞∞———

It was chilly when we all gathered at the university at 6:00 p.m. The take-home test we'd been dreading was finally upon us. We had 24 hours to complete it. The test wasn't going to be easy, but we had a plan: work together, divide the tasks, and hopefully, emerge unscathed.

As soon as we received the test questions, we huddled together for a discussion. The test was divided into two sections: multiple-choice questions and a set of 20 more complex problems.

Sarthak, always good at thinking on his feet, took charge of the MCQs. "I'll handle these." he said, pulling out his laptop. Within minutes, he found answers online, rapidly ticking off one question after another. His efficiency was impressive, and we knew we could rely on him to get those answers right.

The rest of us focused on the remaining 20 questions, which were more challenging, requiring detailed explanations, assumptions and calculations. We worked together for about three hours, exchanging ideas, debating solutions and slowly chipping away at the test. The atmosphere was intense but cooperative; we knew that teamwork was our best shot at success.

However, as the hours passed, the group began to thin out. One by one, people started leaving. Some had jobs to get to, while others were simply too tired to focus any longer.

"I'll pick this up tomorrow." someone said as they packed their things. "Same here." echoed another. Eventually, only a few of us remained.

Govind, who had to work that night, approached me before leaving. "I'll need your help tomorrow morning, Jaideep." he said. "I'm too tired to think straight right now, but I'll meet you first thing in the morning to go over the questions."

I nodded, understanding his predicament. "No worries, I'll be here." I assured him.

I found myself alone in the quiet study room. The clock ticked past 9:00 p.m., and fatigue was setting in, but I couldn't stop now. The thought of the unfinished test gnawed at me. I wouldn't be able to sleep until I'd made more progress.

I decided to burn the midnight oil. I spread out my notes, textbooks and the test questions in front of me, determined to solve as many problems as I could. Hours passed in a blur as I worked through each question, carefully checking and rechecking my answers. By the time I was done, it was well past 2:00 a.m. My eyes were heavy with exhaustion, but I felt a sense of satisfaction. I had answered all the questions to the best of my ability.

The next morning, true to his word, Govind met me at the university. He looked tired but determined. I handed him the solutions I'd worked on the night before.

"Here, these should be good." I said, going over the answers with him. "Just make sure to change a few assumptions so it doesn't look like we copied each other."

Govind nodded, grateful for the help. "Thanks, Jaideep. I'll submit mine after making those changes."

I could barely keep my eyes open, so I headed home. As soon as my head hit the pillow, I drifted off, the stress of the test now forgotten.

But my rest was short-lived. My phone started buzzed incessantly. One after another, the calls came in—my friends, all asking the same questions: "What assumptions did you use? Are you sure the answers are right? What if we get caught?"

Groggy and annoyed, I answered the calls, trying to reassure them. "Look, I'm confident that all my answers are correct. We'll only get caught if the answers are wrong. As long as everything is right, we're in the clear. Just submit the same as mine, but with your names on it. It'll be fine."

Each call ate away at my precious sleep, but I couldn't leave my friends hanging. They trusted me. After the final call, I tossed my phone aside and tried to get back to sleep, though my mind was still racing with thoughts of the test.

Later that day, after some rest, I reflected on the past 24 hours. It had been a whirlwind of stress, cooperation and last-minute cramming. But in the end, we'd all worked together to get through it. Whether or not our answers were perfect, we'd done our best, and that was all we could do.

———∞∞∞∞———

My experience with Traffic Australia was nothing short of exhilarating. The opportunity to travel, explore unknown places and traverse the city from one end to the other was a thrilling adventure. That day brought something new, and I felt like I was part of something bigger, contributing to a project that spanned the entire city. But as exciting as it was, one thing still bothered at me.

In my last conversation with Jaydeep, the team leader, he said, nonchalantly, as if it were just another day at the office. "These kinds of surveys happen all the time across Australia. I'm part of the Victoria team, and so are you—on a casual basis."

That word *casual* struck a nerve. I hated its uncertainty, hated feeling I was just a temporary cog in a much larger machine. I wanted stability, to be a permanent member of the team.

"Is there any chance I can become permanent?" I asked Jaydeep.

He looked at me thoughtfully. "It's possible." he replied, but his tone didn't offer much reassurance. "You just need to keep proving yourself."

Next day, just after submitting the open-book test at university, I received a call from an unknown number. Curious, I answered, and to my surprise, it was a woman from Traffic Australia asking if I'd be interested in working on a part-time basis. My heart raced as I replied with a quick, "Yes."

She told me I'd be paired with Jaydeep again. This was a relief; working with someone familiar made the job less daunting. Together, we embarked on a series of manual surveys that took us all over the city.

The first survey we conducted involved sitting in a car and counting the number of vehicles that passed by a specific point, noting their direction. A simple task, but it needed a keen eye and unwavering concentration. We spent hours in that car, watching the world go by, our notepads filling with numbers and arrows.

Another survey had us standing at a busy intersection, wearing our high-visibility jackets and armed with a speed gun. Our task was to capture the speed at which vehicles passed by and to note their direction. Monotonous work, but it came with its own set of surprises. One day, as I was diligently recording the speed of passing cars, a passerby approached me, curious about my attire and equipment.

"What are you doing here?" he asked. I explained the survey, and he chuckled. "You know, you're all over the internet now. People think you're some cop staking out in broad daylight."

I couldn't help but laugh at the irony. Here I was, just doing my job, and somehow I had become a minor internet sensation. The job wasn't glamorous, but moments like these made it interesting.

Other surveys had their own unique challenges. One day, I found myself standing at a roundabout, marking the point where the longest queue of cars formed within a 15-minute interval on all four sides. The work was repetitive, but again, it required attention to detail. The best part of these jobs was that I was never alone. Whether it was Jaydeep or another team member, we worked together, sharing the workload and the experience.

But then came a task that required only one person. I was assigned to a park, where my job was to count the number of people who entered during a specific timeframe. It felt like a test—a chance to prove my worth to Traffic Australia. I took it seriously, meticulously recording the data so that I didn't miss a single person.

My efforts didn't go unnoticed. After several weeks of proving myself through various assignments, I received a call that was a turning point in my journey with Traffic Australia. It was the same woman who'd first called me for part-time work. This time, she had something more significant to offer.

"We have a big project coming up at Melbourne Airport." she said. "It's a traffic survey, and we need reliable people. The job could involve up to 70 hours of work over two weeks, followed by two weeks off. Are you interested?"

I didn't hesitate. "Absolutely." I said, trying to keep the excitement out of my voice. This was the opportunity I'd been waiting for—a chance to be part of something big, something that could lead to a more permanent role.

After the call, I reflected on how far I'd come since that first conversation with Jaydeep. From casual, part-time work to a potentially career-defining project, my journey with Traffic Australia had been anything but ordinary. The road ahead was still uncertain, but I felt more confident than ever that I was on the right path.

My first day working on the Melbourne Airport project started with Jaydeep meeting me near Glenroy station, close to the airport. As I jumped into the car, I was filled with excitement and anticipation for the day ahead. Jaydeep quickly briefed me about the work and emphasised the importance of this project.

"There are eight teams working on this." he explained. "The days will be long, and we have to install 23 cameras."

"We installed the same number of cameras the other day in just a few hours!"

Jaydeep smiled, shaking his head. "The airport traffic will make the job longer, because travel time from one point to another will take around 30 minutes."

That first day was a marathon. After 12 long hours, we'd only installed 14 cameras. The traffic was relentless, and the sheer size of the airport made every task so time-consuming. As the day ended, Jaydeep said we needed to start early the next day to install the remaining cameras before the scheduled start time.

I dropped Jaydeep at his place and took the car with me so I could come in early the next day, barely catching four hours of sleep before heading back to work. Exhaustion was setting in, but I had to push through. The next day, we managed to install the remaining nine cameras in seven hours. I was drained, my energy sapped from the long hours and relentless pace.

When we finished, I turned to Jaydeep and asked, "Is that all? Is the job done now?"

He smiled, seeing the weariness in my eyes. "We've finished the hard part." he said. "But we still need to be present during the survey to do periodic checks and ensure all the cameras are working. The routine won't change. We'll finish the day late and start early the next morning, but it's an easy job from here on. We can relax and earn money while doing so."

For the next two weeks, all eight teams followed the same routine. We conducted checks, replaced batteries and ensured everything was running smoothly. Despite the long hours, the work was straightforward, and the pressure had eased. There was even a sense of camaraderie among the teams as we settled into the rhythm of the job.

Surprisingly, even though I never got more than five hours of sleep at a stretch during those two weeks, I felt more energetic than ever. The exhaustion I'd felt on the first day was replaced by a sense of purpose. I wasn't done with this job yet—I wanted more. The thrill of the work, the satisfaction of seeing a project come together and the prospect of future travel kept me going.

As the project ended, I found myself eager for the next challenge. I hoped more travelling opportunities would come my way, allowing me to continue exploring new places and taking on new responsibilities. This job had shown me a side of myself I hadn't known before—a resilience and a hunger for adventure that I was excited to pursue further.

In the dim light of my bedroom, the weight of the day's events hung heavy in the air. Sarthak had sent me a message earlier, simple yet chilling: "We need to meet the professor at 5 p.m. It's about the test." I paced back and forth, my mind racing as the clock on the wall ticked ominously towards 5 p.m.

I knew something was wrong. The open 24-hour take-home test was supposed to be straightforward. My heart sank as I considered the possibility that we might have been caught in an act of intentional plagiarism.

At 4:30 p.m., we'd all gathered at the university library. Sarthak, Govind, Sagar and the other seven sat with expressions ranging from anxiety to outright panic. "What do you think this is about?" Sagar asked, her voice trembling slightly.

"I don't know." Deep down, I had a sinking feeling. "But whatever it is, we face it together."

We made our way to the professor's office in silence, each of us lost in our thoughts. When we arrived, Professor Gupta was already waiting, his expression unreadable. He gestured for us to sit and we did so, the tension in the room thick enough to cut with a knife.

"I reviewed your tests." he began, his voice calm but firm. "And while all your answers were correct, I noticed something peculiar. There was a spelling mistake in one of the questions, a missed number, and an additional 'r'—a mistake that none of you should have been able to overlook."

It hit us like a tonne of bricks. We'd all replicated the same error, a mistake that could only have come from a single source.

"This suggests to me." the professor continued, "That there was collaboration in a way that goes beyond what's allowed, or worse, that you all copied from a single source."

He paused, letting his words sink in. "I'm left with two options: either you are expelled, or you fail this subject, wasting six months of your life and $6,000."

The room was silent. I could feel the others' eyes on me, waiting for a response. My mind raced, searching for a way out. Then, an idea struck me.

"Professor." I said, my voice steady despite the anxiety churning inside me, "what if there's a third option?"

Professor Gupta raised an eyebrow, intrigued. "And what would that be?"

"Give us zero on this test." I suggested, "and let us live to fight another day. If we fail because of it, we'll accept the consequences. But if we can recover, we deserve that chance."

The professor leaned back in his chair, considering my proposal. "It's almost the same as the second option." he said slowly. "You won't be able to pass the course with a zero on this test."

"I understand." I replied, meeting his gaze with determination. "But we want that chance. If we fail, we'll face the consequences. But at least let us try."

After a long pause, the professor finally nodded, a slight smile tugging at the corners of his mouth. "Very well. I'll give you that chance. But remember, the outcome is on you."

As we left his office, a mix of relief and uncertainty washed over me. The road ahead was daunting, but for now, we had a fighting chance. And that was enough.

"What can we do now?" Mahesh asked, his voice tinged with concern as we left Professor Gupta's office.

"We need to study harder." I said. "Every day, we'll spend at least two hours solving problems physically, not just reading theory. The other subjects are easier and more theoretical, but this one is definitive and quantitative. We can aim for almost 100 out of 100 in this subject."

I paused, calculating in my head. "This 100-mark test will be converted to 60, so we need to score more than 80 overall to pass. That means we can't afford any more than three mistakes in the final exam."

Mahesh nodded, determination replacing his earlier worry. "So, what's the plan?"

"I'll be at the university every day, focusing on this subject. We'll need to manage our work accordingly and make this our priority."

He sighed, but resolve showed in his eyes. "Let's do it, then. We'll make it happen."

With that, we both knew the road ahead would be tough, but the goal was clear: nothing less than success.

Next week, Jaydeep and I set off from Melbourne early in the morning, the city still wrapped in the quiet of dawn. We were headed to Bendigo to install six traffic cameras and conduct a manual survey over three days.

The drive was smooth, with rolling hills and open fields stretching out before us. Jaydeep, always the conversationalist, filled the car with his usual banter about everything from work to weekend plans. Despite the early hour, his energy was contagious, and by the time we reached Bendigo, I was as alert as ever.

Our first task was to install the six cameras at strategic points around the city. We moved with precision, ensuring each camera was positioned correctly to capture the necessary data. By the time we were done, the sun was high in the sky and the day's heat had set in.

The next three days were a blur of activity. We conducted the manual survey, observing and recording traffic patterns, vehicle counts and pedestrian movements. It was meticulous work, but with Jaydeep's humour lightening the mood, the days passed quickly.

On the final day, we uninstalled the cameras, double-checked our data and prepared to head back to Melbourne. As we drove home, tired but satisfied, Jaydeep turned to me and said, "Another job well done, mate." I couldn't help but agree.

The next two-month period with Traffic Australia and university was a whirlwind, each day packed with the demands of work, travel and study. The routine was intense: Monday through Wednesday were dedicated to lectures and study sessions, where I immersed myself in complex concepts and problem-solving exercises for the third semester's final exams. Professor Gupta was demanding, the coursework was rigorous, but I'd set a high bar for myself. Anything lower than that meant the loss of $6,000 and a waste of six months of my life.

My next job began with a trip to Lakes Entrance, a small town known for its stunning waterways and tranquil atmosphere. As I drove along the winding coastal roads, the early morning sun cast a golden glow over the landscape. The sight of the Gippsland Lakes meeting the ocean was nothing short of breathtaking, and I couldn't help but feel a sense of peace wash over me.

The project in Lakes Entrance was to monitor traffic patterns during the peak tourist season. This was crucial for the town, which relies heavily on tourism. Setting up the equipment near the waterfront, I was constantly reminded of the town's delicate balance between nature and development.

In the evenings, after the day's work was done, I'd take long walks along the beach, the cool breeze carrying the salty scent of the sea, a welcome respite from the intensity of my studies. I found the quiet time by the water helped clear my mind and prepare me for the challenges ahead.

The next week, I travelled inland to Bairnsdale, a town with a rich history and a strong sense of community. The drive took me through lush farmland and rolling hills, with the distant mountains providing a dramatic backdrop. Bairnsdale's charm lay in its blend of old-world architecture and modern amenities, making it a fascinating place to explore.

The work here was to analyse pedestrian movement in the town centre, requiring attention to detail and a deep understanding of how people interacted with their environment. During the day, I worked closely with local authorities, setting up observation points and gathering data. In the evenings, I'd stroll through the town, visiting historical sites such as St Mary's Church with its beautiful murals, or simply enjoying a meal at one of the local cafes. The slower pace of life in Bairnsdale was a stark contrast to the hustle and bustle of my university city, and I found it refreshing.

Next on my itinerary was Traralgon, a town known for its industrial significance and vibrant community. The journey there took me through some of Victoria's most fertile farmland, with vast fields stretching out on either side of the road. As I approached the town, the landscape changed, with the smoke-stacks of power stations rising in the distance, testament to the region's role in powering the state.

In Traralgon, the project was to monitor real-time traffic, par-ticularly during busy peak hours. The challenge here was signifi-cant. Unlike the quieter towns I had visited earlier, Traralgon's traffic patterns were complex, with a mix of local commuters, industrial vehicles and long-distance travellers all vying for space on the roads. My role was to analyse this data and suggest improvements to ease congestion and improve safety.

The workdays were long and demanding, but the town offered its own rewards. In the evenings, I'd explore Traralgon's parks and gardens, or visit the local eateries where the food was hearty and the people friendly. The industrial nature of the town didn't diminish its appeal; rather, it highlighted the resilience and ingenuity of its residents, something I came to admire deeply.

Traralgon was followed by Bendigo—a different experience altogether. The town, with its rich gold-rush history, made me feel I was stepping back in time. The old buildings' grand architecture spoke of a bygone era when the town was one of the richest in the world. The drive to Bendigo was picturesque, with tree-lined roads and small towns that seemed untouched by time.

The Bendigo project was to study traffic management dur-ing peak hours, especially in areas with significant historical landmarks that attracted both locals and tourists. The challenge was to ensure that modern traffic needs didn't interfere with the preservation of these historical sites. The work was fascinating as it required a deep understanding of both urban planning and historical preservation.

After the day's work, I'd spend my evenings exploring the town. I visited the Central Deborah Gold Mine, took a tram ride through the city, and even attended a performance at the historic Capital Theatre. Bendigo's mix of history, culture and modernity was captivating, and I found myself learning not just from my work, but from the town itself.

After that, the Mornington Peninsula was perhaps the most visually stunning of all my destinations. The journey there was a treat in itself, with the road winding along the coast, offering spectacular views of the ocean. The peninsula is known for its wineries, hot springs and beautiful beaches, making it a popular getaway for both locals and tourists.

The project here was particularly demanding: studying the impact of seasonal traffic on the local infrastructure. The peninsula's popularity as a tourist destination meant that traffic could be overwhelming, especially during the summer months. Our task was to analyse the data and come up with solutions to manage this influx without disrupting the natural beauty and tranquillity that the area was known for.

Working in such a beautiful location was both a pleasure and a challenge. The stunning scenery was a constant distraction, but it also inspired me to give my best effort. Each day was a blend of hard work and quiet moments of appreciation for the natural world around me. In the evenings, I'd often find a secluded spot by the beach to study, the sound of the waves providing a soothing background as I went through my notes. The Mornington

Peninsula taught me the importance of balance—between work and rest, between development and preservation.

After that project, the focus shifted back to academia. The exam was looming, and the pressure was immense. My classmates and I often joked about how we were all just trying to survive the semester, but deep down, we knew this was more than just another test—it was the culmination of the results of exposed plagiarism and months of honest hard work.

The days leading up to the exam were a blur of revision, practice questions and late-night study sessions. I filled four notebooks, solved more than 2,000 practice questions, and reviewed every chapter multiple times. I knew the subject inside out, but I still had a nagging doubt—had I done enough?

The exam itself was brutal. The questions were complex, designed to test not just our knowledge, but our understanding and application of concepts. As I worked through each problem, I could feel the weight of the semester bearing down on me. But there was also a sense of calm—I had prepared for this, and I knew I could do it.

No time to relax! Every day was a race against the clock, with bills piling up faster than I could pay them. The instant that money hit my account, it vanished, swallowed by rent, groceries and endless expenses. The stress of making ends meet weighed heavily on me, leaving little room for anything else. I couldn't afford to slow down—not when every dollar counted. The urgency to work, to earn more, became my driving force. It wasn't just about survival; it was about staying afloat in a world that seemed intent on pulling me under.

My next pay came from the Swan Hill project. Swan Hill and Echuca were both located along the Murray River, and both towns had a rich history tied to the river. The drive to these towns was a journey through Victoria's agricultural heartland, with vast expanses of farmland stretching out in all directions.

In Swan Hill, the project involved studying the impact of agricultural transport on the town's infrastructure. The region's reliance on agriculture meant the roads were often filled with large vehicles transporting produce, creating unique challenges for traffic management. The work was hands-on, involving a lot of time in the field, gathering data and talking to local farmers and transport operators.

Echuca, on the other hand, was another town steeped in history, known for its historic port and paddle steamers. The project here was similar but with a focus on balancing tourism and local transport needs. The town's popularity as a tourist destination meant that traffic could be unpredictable, especially during peak holiday seasons.

Both towns offered a glimpse into life along the Murray River, with its unique blend of history, culture and agriculture. I spent my evenings exploring the riverbanks, visiting local museums, and even taking a ride on one of Echuca's famous paddle steamers. The experience was enriching as it combined professional tests with a deep appreciation for the region's history and way of life.

The Great Ocean Road was the following week's project, and it was nothing short of spectacular. The drive along this iconic route is considered one of the most beautiful in the world, with the road hugging the coastline, offering panoramic views of the ocean, cliffs and beaches. As I drove down the winding road, I felt a sense of awe at the sheer beauty of the landscape.

The project was to analyse the traffic-flow along this busy tourist route, particularly in areas where the road was narrow and winding. The test was to find ways to manage the heavy traffic without compromising the safety or natural beauty of the area.

The work was demanding, but the surroundings made it feel less like a job and more like a privilege.

I stayed in small coastal towns along the route, each with its own charm. From the famous Twelve Apostles to the lush rainforests of the Otway Ranges, every stop was a new adventure. In the evenings, I'd sit by the beach with my laptop, going over the day's work and preparing for the next. The sound of the waves, the fresh sea air and the stunning sunsets made it easy to forget the pressures of the project and exam results, and I simply enjoyed it and lived in the present. After the project, I returned home feeling both exhausted and fulfilled, yet anxiously waiting for the results, due the following week.

Early one morning, still groggy with sleep, I was jolted awake by a phone call. The voice on the other end was familiar but unexpected—it was my professor.

"You've done it!" he said, his voice filled with pride. I was confused, unsure if I was still dreaming.

"Who's this?" I croaked.

"It's your professor, Varun Gupta." he replied, his tone warm. "I just finished grading your exam, and I couldn't wait to tell you the results."

My heart raced. "How did I do?"

"You scored 97 out of 100." he said, and I could hear the smile in his voice. "It's the highest score I've ever given. Your understanding of the concepts was exceptional."

For a second, I was speechless. All the hours of study, the late nights, the countless practice questions—it had all paid off.

"Thank you, sir!" I finally managed to say. "I couldn't have done it without your guidance."

He chuckled. "You put in the work. Tell me, how did you prepare?"

I explained my study routine—how I'd dedicated three hours every day to study, how I'd solved more than 2000 practice questions, and filled four notebooks with notes and practice problems.

"That's impressive." he said. "You've set a new standard for excellence."

As I hung up, I felt a deep sense of accomplishment. To me, this was more than just a good grade—it was proof that hard work, dedication and perseverance could overcome any challenge. The third semester had ended with a bang, but it was just the beginning of a new and exciting journey—one that I was ready to embrace with open arms.

The semester had ended, and with it came the promise of a full-time work schedule. I was eagerly waiting for my next project, expecting a call from Traffic Australia at any moment. But as the days turned into weeks, my phone remained silent.

A sense of dread started to creep in—had I done something wrong? Had I made a mistake on one of my previous assignments? The uncertainty gnawed at me, and I began to worry that my opportunity to earn a decent income over the semester break was slipping away.

I needed the money, and I needed it badly. The next four months were my chance to save. Without Traffic Australia, I wasn't sure how I would manage. In desperation, I called their office. The woman on the other end of the line explained why I hadn't received any new projects.

"There are no projects during the holiday season. We won't be resuming work until February."

"*February?*" I echoed. "But it's only October."

"Yes, we're shut for four months." she said. "We'll call you if anything comes up."

I thanked her and hung up, feeling both disappointment and panic. Four months without work? I couldn't afford that. The prospect of going back to odd jobs such as washing cars or working at a convenience store filled me with dread. I'd grown accustomed to the challenges and rewards of my work with Traffic Australia, and the thought of returning to more menial tasks felt like a step backwards.

But much as I wanted to be selective, I knew survival didn't allow for such luxuries. I had to keep pushing through these tough times, no matter how disheartening they were. I started scouring job listings again, but my heart wasn't in it. I didn't want to go back to what I had been doing before. I wanted more.

Just when I was starting to lose hope, luck intervened unexpectedly. Rohit called out of the blue. He was going to India for a few months and needed someone to take care of his bike while he was away.

"Can I use it?" I asked.

"Of course." he replied. "No need to ask."

Suddenly, a new opportunity opened up. With Rohit's bike, I could get back to doing Uber Eats deliveries. It wasn't Traffic Australia, but it was something, and it would keep me going until February when work resumed. The relief I felt was overwhelming. I stopped my job hunt and shifted my focus to setting up for delivery work.

All my friends had gone to India to visit their families, and I was the only one left behind. I couldn't go back to see my family because I simply didn't have the money. Determined to make the most of my situation, I decided to work as much as I could for Uber Eats.

November was a great month. The weather was amazing, and with fewer student delivery drivers around, I could snag orders quickly and earn more. The city was alive, the air was crisp and I was making decent money. Everything seemed to be going well.

But then December arrived, and things changed. The weather was still great, with longer days and plenty of sunshine, but when the weather is good, everyone wants to go out to eat. Nobody orders delivery. I spent my days just roaming the streets, hoping for an order to come through, but the days were slow and the earnings even slower. January was more of the same. Despite my best efforts, I barely made enough to get by.

As February rolled around, things started to look up. Orders began to pick up, and I finally felt like I was getting back on track.

But just as I was beginning to see a glimmer of hope, Rohit returned from India. He wanted his bike back, and without it, my ability to do deliveries vanished.

By that time, I had exhausted all my savings and hadn't earned nearly as much as I had hoped. The stress was mounting, and I wasn't sure how I was going to make it through the rest of the break.

Just when I thought things couldn't get any worse, I received an unexpected call from Traffic Australia. They said work would resume in March, and they needed me to test all the equipment to ensure that the projects would go smoothly.

It was the lifeline I desperately needed. Though the past few months had been tough, the prospect of getting back to work with Traffic Australia gave me a renewed sense of purpose.

As the final semester approached, the pressure to choose a thesis topic began to weigh on my mind. I knew I wanted a subject that not only aligned with my academic goals, but also leveraged my previous work experience.

After much thought, I decided on "Integrating IT with supply chain management" as my topic. I was genuinely interested in this area, and I felt confident my background would give me a strong foundation for the research.

I scheduled a meeting with my professor to discuss the idea. Walking into his office, I felt a mix of excitement and nerves. This was a crucial step in my academic journey, and I wanted to make sure I conveyed the significance of my chosen topic.

"Good morning, Professor." I said, taking a seat across from him.

"Good morning. So, what have you decided for your thesis?" he asked, leaning back in his chair.

"I've been thinking about focusing on the integration of IT with supply chain management." I said. "It's an area I'm familiar with, especially after my work experience at Bajaj Electricals Limited in India. There, I was involved in several projects that required a deep understanding of both IT systems and supply chain processes."

The professor listened intently, nodding as I spoke. "That's an interesting topic." he said. "With the increasing reliance on technology in supply chain operations, this could be a very relevant and impactful study."

"I believe so, too." I replied. "My experience at Bajaj has given me insight into the practical challenges and opportunities in this area. I think it will allow me to contribute something valuable to the existing body of research."

The professor smiled, pleased with my choice. "I see you've put a lot of thought into this. I'm confident you'll do well. Consider your thesis topic approved."

Relief washed over me, and I felt a renewed sense of purpose. This was the culmination of everything I had worked for, and I was ready to meet the challenge.

My thesis subject became my sole focus for the semester. With no lectures to attend and no attendance requirements, I was free to work to my own schedule. This allowed me to balance my thesis research with work at Traffic Australia, now slowly picking up pace.

Each week, I eagerly awaited the next work schedule, ready to travel to various locations. The first assignment took me to Mt Baw Baw for three days. It was the off-season, so the place was nearly deserted, offering an unparalleled sense of serenity and peace. As we reached the summit of the mountain, I wished the entire world could be this tranquil. The crisp mountain air, the silence broken only by the rustling of leaves and the breathtaking views all around made it an unforgettable experience.

After Mt Baw Baw, my work took me to Taggerty, a small town surrounded by lush forests and flowing rivers. The drive itself was a treat, with winding roads and picturesque landscapes at every turn. The work was difficult, but the natural beauty of the area made it all worthwhile.

Next was a three-day project in Ballarat. Known for its rich history and well-preserved architecture, Ballarat offered a stark contrast to the tranquillity of Mt Baw Baw. The town was bustling with activity, yet a quieter charm prevailed in its streets lined with old buildings and cafes. My time there was productive, and I appreciated the blend of history and modernity that Ballarat offered.

The following week, I headed to Portland, a coastal town known for its rugged beauty and historic significance as one of Victoria's oldest European settlements. The ocean's proximity provided a refreshing change of pace, and I spent my evenings walking along the beach, watching the waves crash against the shore. The sound of the ocean was both calming and invigorating, a perfect end to long days of work.

As the weeks passed, each new destination brought with it unique experiences and challenges. The constant travel kept things interesting, and I found that the varied environments fuelled my creativity and focus on my thesis. The peacefulness of Mt Baw Baw, the natural beauty of Taggerty, the historical charm of Ballarat and the coastal serenity of Portland all contributed to a growing sense of contentment and purpose.

My thesis began to take shape during these travels. My schedule's flexibility allowed me to focus on my research, and I began to draw connections between my academic work and the practical experiences I was gaining in the field. The integration of IT with supply chain management became more than just a topic; it was a living, breathing project that evolved with each new location I visited.

After a month of travelling for work, I was asked to switch gears and work in the office to help with some analysis. The change of pace was welcome, and I found myself enjoying the camaraderie of the office. Collaborating with colleagues, bouncing ideas off one another and engaging in lively discussions brought a new dimension to my work.

However, as much as I appreciated the dynamic atmosphere of the office, I did miss the field trips: something about being in different locations, experiencing new surroundings and the sense of freedom that came with it. The quiet times of reflection in remote areas and the thrill of discovery were aspects of the job that the office, despite its comforts, simply couldn't replicate.

While the analytical work was engaging and crucial for our projects, I often found myself longing for the open roads, the scenic landscapes, and the challenges that came with on-site work. The balance between the office and the field had shifted, and though I understood the importance of the analysis, a part of me longed to return to the field, where every day brought a new adventure.

A significant project came up, one that required our entire team to mobilise. We were to carry equipment from the Melbourne office to Adelaide, embarking on a week-long project that promised to be both stimulating and exciting. The plan was straightforward: load up the gear, hit the road, complete the work and drive back. What I didn't anticipate was just how memorable this journey would be.

The road trip to Adelaide was one of the best experiences. The open road, the camaraderie of a shared journey and the promise of new sights that make these trips special. Our route took us through some of the most stunning landscapes in southern Australia, and with every kilometre the anticipation grew.

One of the highlights of the trip was our visit to the Pink Lake. Nestled off the beaten path, this natural wonder lived up to its name, with the water glowing a surreal shade of pink. Standing by the shore, I felt awed by the sheer beauty of nature. It was one of those times that stays with you long after the trip is over.

Another standout was our stop at Mt Gambier. Known for its volcanic landscape and the famous Blue Lake, Mount Gambier offered a completely different kind of beauty. The vibrant blue of the lake, contrasted against the lush green surroundings, was breathtaking. We took some time to explore the area, appreciating the unique geological features that made this place so special.

As we continued our journey, we passed through small towns and vast stretches of countryside, each with its own appeal. Every stop along the way added to the richness of the experience, making the road trip as rewarding as the project itself.

By the time we reached Adelaide, we were both exhausted and exhilarated. The week was intense, filled with long hours and hard work, but the satisfaction of completing such a significant project made it all worthwhile. The drive back to Melbourne was quieter, with everyone reflecting on the journey and the work we'd accomplished. This trip wasn't just about reaching a destination; it was about the experience, the places we saw, and the memories we'd created along the way.

The following month, we were awarded a project in rural New South Wales. This was my first opportunity to travel there and the excitement was substantial. The project required us to drive from Melbourne all the way to Singleton, a small town located about 200 km north of Sydney—a long journey, but one that I eagerly anticipated.

We set out early in the morning, the car packed with equipment and the team in high spirits. As we left Melbourne behind and hit the open road, I felt a sense of adventure. The scenery was nothing short of spectacular. Rolling hills, and vast plains, and the occasional glimpse of the ocean kept us company as we made our way north.

As we approached the outskirts of Sydney, the landscape began to change. The air grew warmer and the greenery more lush. Then we were greeted by a sight that took my breath away— a double rainbow stretching across the sky. The colours were so vivid, and the arc of the rainbow seemed to reach down to the road ahead of us. For a while, it felt as if we were driving straight towards it, as if it was a gate welcoming us to our destination.

The beauty of the scene was almost surreal. The rainbows seemed to envelop us, creating an impression of pure magic, as though Nature itself was celebrating our arrival, marking the start of what I knew would be a memorable experience. We paused to take in the view, the team sharing in the awe of the spectacle. It felt like a good omen, a sign that this project was going to be something special.

The rest of the drive to Singleton was filled with a sense of anticipation. As we passed through the outskirts of Sydney, I marvelled at the city's skyline in the distance, its iconic landmarks silhouetted against the evening sky. But our journey didn't end there. We continued north, leaving the bustling city behind as we headed into the quieter, more rural parts of New South Wales.

Singleton, with its rolling vineyards and picturesque countryside, was a world away from the urban sprawl of Sydney. The town had a charm of its own, with tree-lined streets and a slower pace of life—a fitting contrast to the excitement of the drive and the grandeur of the rainbows we'd seen earlier.

Over the next few days, we focused on the project, completing it with the same dedication and precision that had become our hallmark. But even as we worked, the memory of that rainbow stayed with me—a reminder of the beauty to be found in unexpected places, and a symbol of hope and promise.

At sunset, as we were driving back to Melbourne, Jaydeep and I reflected on the past year. The long hours on the road had a way of opening up conversations, and this time, our talk turned to the many places I'd visited with Traffic Australia.

"You've really covered some ground this past year." Jaydeep remarked, glancing over at me as he steered the car along the winding road.

I nodded, a smile tugging at the corners of my mouth. "Yeah, it's been quite the journey. I never imagined I'd get to see so much of Victoria, let alone in such a short time."

Jaydeep chuckled. "You've been everywhere, haven't you? From Mt Baw Baw to Portland, and now all the way up to Adelaide in South Australia and Singleton in New South Wales. That's not something most people get to do, especially while working."

I leaned back in my seat, feeling contentment wash over me. "I know. I'm really grateful for the opportunities Traffic Australia has given me. It's been more than just work—it's been an experience, a chance to see parts of the state I might never have visited otherwise."

Jaydeep glanced over at me again, a thoughtful expression on his face. "You know, not everyone gets to do what you've done. Travel, work and still manage to study and keep up with everything else. It's impressive."

I shrugged, feeling a bit embarrassed by the praise. "I've just been lucky. But yeah, it's been incredible. Each place has its own vibe, its own story. I feel like I've learned as much from the road as I have from any textbook."

We drove in silence for a while, the quiet hum of the car filling the space between us. Finally, as we reached Melbourne, he said, "You've passed through or been at every city council in Victoria, you know that?"

A CALCULATED SACRIFICE

"You're really enjoying your job at Traffic Australia." Rigved remarked after I finished telling him about the past 12 months of juggling constant travel and university studies. With our work schedules, catching up had become almost impossible. Any time outside of work was dedicated to studying for exams, and later, my thesis.

"Yeah, I am enjoying it." I replied. "But last week, we ended up on the same project again. I asked Jaydeep if we'd get to see any new places, but he said, this is it. There are only two traffic surveying companies, and both have their territories marked out. So, no more new places. As much as I love travelling for work, I don't want to keep revisiting the same spots."

"So, what's your plan, now you've finished your master's?"

"I submitted my final thesis two weeks ago, after returning from Sydney. The presentation went smoothly, and the panel seemed satisfied with my work. Now, I'm just waiting for the results, which should be out in couple of months. My student visa will expire soon, so I applied for a graduate visa yesterday."

"How long is the graduate visa valid for?" Rigved asked.

"Two years."

"What will you do if you don't get the graduate visa before the student visa expires?"

"In that case, my bridging visa will be activated until the result on my graduate visa application."

"Are you thinking of going back home or staying here?"

"I'm not planning on going back just yet. I'll start looking for a white-collar job, and once I land *the* job, I'll begin the PR process."

"And what's *the* job?"

"I guess I'll know it when I find it."

"Do you realise it's not that easy to find a job that leads to permanent residency? You need references and local experience in a similar field. Overseas experience doesn't count, and local blue-collar experience on a temporary visa doesn't either."

"So, what do you suggest? Give up?"

"No, not at all. I'd suggest looking for an internship. It might pay less, but it'll offer better long-term prospects."

"My classmate during my masters, Kunal just started an internship in Sydney. I'll ask him if any opportunities are available." I picked up my phone and called him, but no answer. "He must be at the office." I said, putting the phone down.

Later that day, Kunal called back. "Hey, you called?"

"Yeah, just wanted to check in—how's the internship going?"

"It's going well. There are ten interns here, all Europeans. It's a lot of fun. They offer jobs after the internship too, so I'm hoping there'll be openings when I'm done."

"Nice. And how's life in Sydney?"

"Busy, really busy."

"Sounds good. I'm also looking for jobs in Sydney, so I thought I'd check if there are any internship opportunities where you are."

"Actually, there's one in the Product Management team. One of the interns backed out at the last minute, so they're urgently looking to fill the spot."

"Could you recommend me?"

"Sure thing. Send me your resume and I'll do it as soon as they're back from lunch."

"Thanks, Kunal. Talk to you soon."

That afternoon, I received a call from an unknown number.

"Hi Jaideep, this is Roger. I got your contact from Kunal. He mentioned you're interested in an internship."

"Yes, I am. I just finished my master's in engineering management and I'm looking for a full-time opportunity. I think gaining some local experience through an internship would be very helpful."

"If we decide to select you, how soon could you start?"

"I can start immediately. I'm not tied to a notice period at my current job, and I live in shared accommodation. The owner is quite understanding and will support my situation."

"Could you join in ten days?"

"Yes, absolutely."

"Great. In that case, I'm going to put you on speaker. Consider this an interview. Are you ready?"

"I am not mentally prepared for this." I said, "but I'll give it a shot. Will I get another chance if I don't do well now?"

"Don't worry, I won't ask the usual questions about strengths, weaknesses or where you see yourself in five years—none of that nonsense. Let's get straight to the point."

"Okay."

"I've seen your resume. It's impressive. Why are you looking for an internship then?"

"I moved from India two years ago and just finished my master's. I've applied for many jobs, but I keep hitting a wall when it comes to providing references or local experience. My goal with this internship is to integrate into the Australian workforce—learn the office culture, work style, language, customs and everything else. I'm confident I can handle the work itself."

"On a scale of 1 to 10, how confident are you with Excel?"

"I'd rate myself a nine. Aside from macros, I'm familiar with everything needed."

"We don't need macros here, anyway. Do you know Pivot Tables and VLOOKUP?"

"Yes."

"Can you explain VLOOKUP?"

"I can try. Could I explain it with an example?"

"Go ahead."

"Let's say we have the points scored by individual players in two different tabs of an Excel workbook, and we want to bring those into two different columns of a worksheet. We can use the player's name as the lookup value, the second scorecard as the table array, set the column index number to 2, and finish with 'false' for an exact match."

"Good. Correct. Why 'false'?"

"I'm not entirely sure, but I was taught it should always be 'false' to ensure we get the exact value."

"That's true. No pun intended." Roger replied. "That's it for the interview. As far as I'm concerned, you're selected, but the manager would like to have a word with you." He put her on.

"Hi Jaideep, this is Hafiza. I'm the Head of Product Management. How are you?"

"I'm good, thank you. How are you?"

"I have to say, this was the quickest interview I've ever been part of, and an even quicker selection. But don't give yourself all the credit. We made such a quick decision because Roger, our current intern, has to leave in a month. We need someone to start within two weeks so he can train you and pass the torch. I support his decision, and he's given me a thumbs-up to confirm that you know your way around Excel. Just one thing: we only pay $1,200 a month to interns." She paused to let that sink in. "Are you still interested?"

"Yes, I am."

"Think it through. Sydney is an expensive city. You're used to Melbourne prices."

"I understand. But I don't have much of a choice. I need to start my career somewhere, and this is a good starting point. It'll be tough, but I'm ready for it."

"I'll ask HR to send you a contract. Be prepared to travel in a week's time. Congratulations, Jaideep. See you soon."

"Thank you very much."

Within a few minutes I received an email from the HR team with an internship contract. Without any delay I signed it and sent it back before they changed their mind.

The next day, I called my manager at Traffic Australia.

"Hey, I just wanted to let you know that I'm heading to Sydney for an internship." I said. "Please keep me in mind if any permanent jobs open up at Traffic Australia."

He asked, "Would you prefer field jobs or office work?"

"I'd prefer office jobs." I replied.

During our conversation, I also asked, "Is it possible for me to get shifts every day this week? I need to earn as much as I can since the internship won't pay much."

"Sure, we can arrange that." he agreed. "Come to the office every day."

With that settled, we disconnected the call, and I started packing for Sydney.

For the next eight days, I worked continuously, saving hard. After saying goodbye to all my friends in Melbourne, I boarded a Greyhound overnight bus to Parramatta, where I was to stay with Kunal.

I'd managed to save $2,000, which I brought with me to Sydney along with two bags. Upon arrival, I had to pay a $700 deposit and $700 for the first month's rent, leaving me with just $600. When I reached Sydney, Kunal said I wouldn't get paid until next month. My daily commute would cost $175, each month and I had an iPhone 6s on a contract with Vodafone from a year ago, which required a $155 monthly payment. On top of that, my mandatory medical insurance, Medibank, cost me $100 per month.

This meant I was left with just $170 to cover all my expenses, including clothing, food and trying to maintain some semblance of a life. And when I finally get paid $1,200 next month, I'd only have $70 left for personal expenses, including food.

In the first week of my internship, I made some European friends. It was exciting to meet people from different nationalities, learn about their lifestyles, hang out with them, share laughs and enjoy the time. However, every good thing comes with a price, and within two weeks, I'd exhausted my minimal savings.

When my first pay arrived, I felt relieved. But with my new budget, I could only afford to spend $70 a month on food. To make it work, I devised an ingenious solution. Each month, I would buy 5kg of rice for $15, half a litre of cooking oil for $7, 2kg of onions for $5, and 2kg of tomatoes in four lots for $8—$2 per lot. This plan allowed me to save $35. Each day, I could buy cans of chickpeas, kidney beans or lentils for 80 cents and still save seven to eight dollars, depending on the number of days in the month. Meat would be off the menu for the foreseeable future.

Still, my finances went from bad to worse. The thought of borrowing money crossed my mind, but my ego got in the way. Besides, I knew everyone else was struggling too; no point in asking for help.

Each day seemed to hit a new low, so I stopped checking my bank account to avoid sinking into depression. I even started fasting on Saturdays, hoping to either gain some goodwill from God or just to save a bit more money.

On the Sunday after one of my fasting days, I went to Coles to buy my monthly groceries. I scanned the tomatoes, onions and rice, then proceeded to pay. But my card was declined due to insufficient funds. I closed my eyes, swallowed hard and lowered my head, absorbing yet another blow. I braced myself to apologise to the staff for the inconvenience of having to return the items to the shelves.

I looked around and I saw I was alone at the self-service station. No one was in sight. I was starving, having only had water the day before, and I desperately needed these groceries to get through the week. I hesitated for a few seconds, but with no other option, I put all the items in my bag and walked out without paying.

This became a regular thing now. To cope with my guilt, I started praying harder. "God, please forgive me for this. I promise, once I'm back on my feet, I'll repay this by giving it all back as charity."

But things just kept getting worse. One evening, Kunal came home with some news.

"Guess what? I got the permanent job! Same company, same role." he said, grinning from ear to ear.

"That's amazing, man! I'm really happy for you." I replied, with a smile. This gave me hope that someday I'd get out of this financial burden, too.

But then he added, "There's one more thing. I'm moving to a new place."

"Oh! Where to?" I asked, trying to hide my concern.

"Randwick, it's closer to work."

I hesitated, then said, "That's great for you, but ... I think I'll stay here. I can't really afford anything more right now."

Kunal nodded, understanding my situation, and we both fell silent, the reality of our different paths sinking in. After some time he asked, "So, what's your plan to get out of this financial mess?"

I sighed, "I've been applying for part-time jobs with weekend shifts only, but no luck so far. Usually, the permanent staff take the weekend shifts because they get paid more on those days. I've also been messaging the Last Man Stands' Sydney manager every week, asking if there are any umpiring gigs available. Hopefully, I'll get some chances soon."

Kunal nodded sympathetically. "I hope something comes through for you soon."

A couple of weeks later, I was alone in a giant, empty three-bedroom house with timber floors. The sound of my own footsteps echoed eerily, making me feel like I was a character in a horror movie. I only had two pictures of God to keep me company, and I found myself talking to them like a madman.

"Please, help me get through this." I would murmur. "I'm doing my best. Just give me a sign, anything."

Going out only made things worse because I'd see things I wanted to buy but couldn't afford, making me even more miserable. I started staying home, hoping that somewhere, somehow, God was listening to me. If I kept talking to those photos, maybe something would change.

And then, it did!

One day, I got a call from Last Man Stands. "Are you available to umpire this weekend? Four matches, $50 per match, total $200."

"I'm in!"

Soon after, a guy showed up at my place and handed me a kit for umpiring. Finally, a glimmer of hope.

Every weekday, I spent my time in the office, continuing my internship and trying to distract myself from the tension of debts. I couldn't see any light at the end of the tunnel, but I was putting in the effort to get noticed and hopefully secure a full-time position.

One day, deep in my work, my phone rang. It was Laura, sales manager from ANL (Australian National Line). We were her customer. "Hey, what's the status of that quote I gave you two weeks back?" she asked.

I quickly checked the details and replied, "I'll get back to you ASAP."

I then called the person I'd forwarded the quote to. He answered, "I'm placing a booking now."

Relieved, I called Laura back. "We're placing the booking now on the quote you provided."

She sounded surprised. "That was quick!"

I laughed a little, "Didn't you ask for it?"

"Yes, I did. Thank you!! I was just kidding." she replied with a chuckle.

Feeling a bit embarrassed, I said, "Oh, sorry! I'm new to Australia's work culture. I haven't quite figured out the work humour yet."

"No worries at all." she said, still amused. "Let me know if you need anything else."

"Will do. Thanks, Laura."

I was looking forward to this weekend, knowing I'd be earning $200 in a single day by umpiring. Excitement got me out of bed early. I left home, caught the bus and arrived at the ground 30 minutes before the first game. The teams showed up on time, and the match began right on schedule.

The first ball was a gem—a perfect delivery, swinging in and missing the bat, hitting the pad. It was plumb, and I raised my finger for the out within three seconds. The batsman cursed me as he walked off, but I remembered the first thing I was taught in cricket umpiring: every batsman thinks he's not out, and every bowler thinks it's a wicket every time they appeal. So, I brushed off the urge to react and focused on the next ball.

The second ball was almost identical to the first, with the same outcome. This time, I was greeted with a stare from the batsman. The fielding team appreciated me for making the tough call.

Then came the third ball—new batsman, similar delivery, but this time drifting down the leg side. I judged it not out. The bowler, eager for a hat trick, muttered a few unpleasant words, clearly unhappy with my decision.

This experience taught me a valuable lesson about perspective. Humans are wired to see things from their own point of view, and that perspective can shift instantly depending on the situation.

After the first three eventful balls, the first game finished on time. The second game was uneventful, moving at an easy pace, but it still added $50 to my account. The third game delayed the fourth, and by the time the last match began, I was exhausted. When it ended, I was done for the day.

I packed my kit bag and waited 20 minutes for the bus. When I checked, I saw it was cancelled. I couldn't afford an Uber, and the house was 7 km away. It was still hot, and my legs were tired from standing all day. The station was 4 km away, but even after getting off the train, I'd still have to walk another 1.2 km, so, I decided to walk the full 7 km and save money.

It took me two hours to reach home, with several stops along the way. Standing all day and then walking with 7 kg on my back made it a tough journey. But as soon as I got home, the cold shower, a meal and a good night's sleep made it all worthwhile.

Two weeks passed without much thought, and my financial situation began to improve. I started earning almost 80 percent more than before. It wasn't a huge amount, but it brought me some peace of mind, and I could finally afford to have meat again. I paid off all my Vodafone debt, and my weekends became busier, leaving little time to dwell on the shortcomings in my life. Umpiring helped me stay focused on the present.

One day, I arrived at the office, and before I could even put my bag down and settle into my cubicle, my manager called me into her office. I knew it would be my internship review, when I'd find out if I had a shot at a job here. With a mix of hope and anxiety, I walked into her office.

"How's your internship going?" she asked.

"It's going well." I replied. "I've learned a lot and developed good connections, both professionally and personally. But I know I haven't always shown a positive attitude because of financial stress and not being in the best frame of mind."

She nodded, "I've noticed that, too. You don't always seem confident in your work."

"I'm aware." I admitted. "That's largely due to the issues I mentioned. But despite that, I've met all my deadlines over the past four months. I've handled the workload even when you were on trips, and I've gone beyond what was required."

"You've handled the department well since Hafiza's departure. You've relieved a lot of pressure on the director, and he
appreciates it, but we're looking for someone who is a senior and
can command respect."

"I understand." I said. "I know I can do more, but I need a
fair chance—one where I'm not constantly worrying about other
things, so I can fully focus on my work."

She responded, "There will always be something in life that
puts pressure on you and impacts your work. It's not a reason for
poor performance; it's just an excuse."

I felt a bit defensive. "First of all, it's not poor performance.
Statistically, I've done better than what was required. The issue
is with my attitude, which is subjective. If you knew what it's
like to constantly receive calls from companies and friends asking for owed money, you'd understand. Just last month, I got
a call from a debt recovery agency because I'd defaulted on so
many Vodafone payments. It's hard to stay positive under those
circumstances."

She softened, "Fair enough. If I am being honest with you,
we're moving most of our jobs offshore, and we're not sure what
will happen after the full transition. There's currently a hiring
freeze. I'd suggest you start looking for jobs now, so by the time
your internship ends in two months, you'll either have something
lined up or at least a possibility."

After this short yet definitive conversation, I returned to my
desk, completed my daily tasks with a sense of urgency, and then
jotted down the names of the 11 good professional contacts I'd
developed over the past four months. With the list in hand, I
stepped outside the office and made my first call.

"Hi, Laura." I began, "how are you doing?" We exchanged
pleasantries, then I got to the point. "I'll be finishing my internship

in two months, but unfortunately, there are no vacancies here, and there's a hiring freeze. So, I'm calling to ask if there are any job opportunities at ANL?"

"This is a good time to call." she replied, which was music to my ears. "We're actually looking for a sales-support representative, and based on our previous experience, I think you'd be a good fit for the role." She paused, and then there was silence.

"Hello, are you still there?" I asked.

"Sorry." she said, "I was just looking for that email from HR. I can't find it right now, but send me your resume, and I'll forward it to the HR team."

"Thanks, I'll send it in 15 minutes." I assured her.

"Just a word of caution." she added, "don't hold your breath for this. Our HR team is slow, and it might take a while for them to get back to you."

"Not a problem. Thanks for the heads-up."

After that call, I contacted the remaining ten people on my list. They all asked me to send my resume and encouraged me to keep in touch.

By this time, I was really missing my family. I'd been so focused on chasing my dream that I didn't think about the simple things that truly made me happy. I didn't even get it when the experience of leaving home to fulfil a dream had transformed into the dream of going back home. But returning without a job felt like failure, so I kept pushing forward.

Inspiration can come from one of the most unexpected places. One day, talking with Govind, he said, "Go home for a while. Refresh your mind and come back. By the time you return, you'll have a job." He even offered to help with the flight tickets. After our conversation, I booked my flights.

In the following weeks, my routine became a cycle of work, weekend umpiring and relentless job applications. Each application felt like running into the same wall—most positions higher than internships were full-time roles, and my visa had only a year and a half left. Despite this, I pressed on, taking it one step at a time.

Then, just a week before my internship ended and three weeks before my flight to India, I received a call from ANL's HR team. They wanted me to come in the next day for an interview. The opportunity felt like a lifeline, so I began preparing in earnest, knowing this could be a crucial step forward.

All that evening and early morning before reaching the office, I practised by answering all possible interview questions to prepare for it. Feeling rejuvenated, I got ready and headed to the office for my interview.

"Hello, I'm here for an interview with Sheila." I told the receptionist. She made a quick call, then hung up and pointed to the sofa. "Please have a seat."

I sat down, mentally rehearsing my answers. My eyes fell on a newspaper on the table. Thinking it might be useful to reference some current affairs during the interview, I picked it up and, as usual, flipped straight to the last page.

The headline screamed in big, bold letters: *Caught on Tape: Sandpapergate.* Shocked, I read the first line—**Australian Cricketers Caught in Ball Tampering Using Sandpaper.** My mind was blown, and I was engrossed in the article when I heard, "Hey, hi, Jaideep."

I almost wanted to say, "Hold on." but I quickly responded, "Hi, Sheila. Good morning!"

She asked me to follow her into a meeting room. "We'll be joined by Gabriela, our HR head, and Jane, our National Sales Manager, online from Melbourne for this interview."

The first question was, as anticipated: "Tell us about yourself."

With a smile, I began, "My name is Jaideep, born and raised in Mumbai, India. After completing my bachelor's in electrical engineering, I worked as a supply chain analyst at an electrical equipment trading company in India for two years. To advance my career, I decided to pursue a master's in engineering, which brought me to Australia. I recently completed my master's with a specialisation in supply chain management from RMIT University, Melbourne City Campus. During my studies, I realised that Australia is predominantly an importing country, and I had no experience in international supply chain. So, after finishing my master's, I sought an entry-level position in the freight-forwarding industry. I secured an internship in the Ocean Product Management department, where I gained insight into ocean network operations. Now, with my internship ending in two weeks, I'm looking for a full-time position."

Jane then asked, "Why didn't they offer you a full-time position after your internship?"

"They're currently offshoring some jobs, and there's a hiring freeze. They're unsure which roles will remain here, so they didn't hire me. Also, as an intern, the pay wasn't great, which added financial pressure that affected my performance."

The interview continued with the usual questions—nothing too technical. But my mind kept drifting back to the sandpaper scandal. I couldn't focus, and I felt like I wasn't giving satisfactory answers.

At the end, the HR representative said, "We'll inform you of the progress in three weeks."

I replied, "Thank you. I'm heading to India in three weeks, so if you can't reach me by phone, please email me."

I left the interview room and headed straight to my internship office. Once there, I immediately dived into my daily tasks. As soon as I finished, my manager approached me.

"How was the interview?" she asked.

"It didn't go very well." I admitted. "The first couple of questions were fine, but then my mind kept drifting back to that sandpaper incident in the newspaper. I just couldn't focus on the interview."

She gave me a sympathetic look, probably thinking I was an idiot. "That's okay." she said. "It's just your first opportunity. Learn from this and make sure it doesn't happen again next time."

"Yeah, I will." I replied, though I couldn't shake the feeling that I wouldn't be selected after this interview. "I still need to keep looking for jobs."

After our discussion, we broke for lunch, and I shared the details of my interview with my other intern friends.

During the last week of my internship, my focus had completely shifted from completing daily tasks to applying for jobs online. I was constantly on Seek.com and LinkedIn, and I called all my professional contacts.

One day, my manager said, "You seem preoccupied."

"Yeah, I've been applying for jobs non-stop." I replied. "With the umpiring gigs, I've saved up a little money, so at least I'm not stressed about my finances anymore.

"That's good to hear." she said, with an encouraging smile.

After finishing my internship, I returned to work for Traffic Australia in Sydney on a casual basis. They were kind enough to offer me roles for two weeks. One day, I confided in a colleague.

"I'm desperately waiting for a call from ANL." I said. "But honestly, I'm not holding my breath. After that interview, I'm pretty sure I won't be selected."

"Sometimes things work out when you least expect them to." he said.

Two days before my departure to India, I decided to call Gabriele about my application.

"Hi Gabriele, it's Jaideep. I was wondering if there's any update on the job at ANL?" I asked, trying to keep my voice steady.

"Hi Jaideep! You're actually the frontrunner for the job." she said, to my surprise. "However, the scope has changed. It's now a one-year contract role instead of a full-time position. But there's potential for the contract to be extended or even become a full-time role."

"That's great news." I replied, feeling relieved. "With my visa only valid for another year and a half, a one-year contract fits perfectly. I'll work on my PR as soon as I get the job. This opportunity really aligns with my situation."

"I'm glad to hear that, Jaideep." she said. "We'll be in touch soon."

As I was wrapping up the call with Gabriele, I mentioned, "Just a heads-up, I'm leaving for India in two days and will be back in three weeks."

"Thanks for letting me know. I'll do my best to get you an update before you leave. But if the decision isn't made within these two days, I'll make sure to send you an email."

"Perfect, thanks, Gabriele." I said, more reassured.

The next day, at exactly 9 a.m., my phone rang: Gabriele. The promptness of the call startled me—almost as if she had been waiting for the clock to strike nine. As I saw her name on the screen, a wave of anxiety rushed over me. My first thought was that she was calling to reject my application, figuring that her first task of the day was to filter out candidates. I had mentally prepared myself for this, but actually facing it was a different story.

Despite my nerves, I answered the call with a positive tone. After greetings, she said, "I'm calling to let you know that you've been selected for the second round of interviews."

Relief washed over me, and I couldn't help but smile. "That's great! Is it online, or do you need me there in person?" I asked.

"What's more suitable for you?"

"I need to pack all my things for tomorrow, so I'd prefer an online interview." She agreed, and I quickly followed up, "Could we do it today?"

"How about this afternoon?"

"That works for me!" I said, feeling a mix of excitement and urgency.

Within 15 minutes, an email confirmed the interview at 12:30 p.m. for 45 minutes.

As the clock struck 12:30, I logged into the video call, taking a deep breath to calm my nerves. The screen flickered and soon, Gabriele, Sheila and Jane appeared. They greeted me warmly, which helped ease some of my anxiety.

"Hi Jaideep, thank you for joining us on such short notice." Gabriele started. "We appreciate your flexibility."

"Thank you for the opportunity."

Sheila took the lead, "We were impressed with your background and the experience you gained during your internship. Today, we'd like to delve deeper into how you handle specific challenges, particularly in a fast-paced environment like ours."

The questions that followed were more focused and technical, unlike the first round. Jane asked about specific scenarios—how I would handle multiple deadlines, manage client expectations or respond to an unexpected issue in the supply chain.

At first, I felt a little shaky.

One question stood out: "Tell us about a time when you had to make a tough decision under pressure. How did you handle it, and what was the outcome?"

I took a second, then decided to talk about my umpiring experience. "During one of the matches I umpired, I had to make a series of tough calls right at the start. The bowler was on fire, and the first two balls had the batsmen trapped LBW (leg before wicket), but on the third, I had to judge that the ball was missing leg stump, despite the bowler's appeal. The fielding team wasn't happy, and it was difficult to stay composed with everyone watching. But I knew I had to make the right call, and I did. The experience taught me to trust my judgment and stay calm under pressure."

Both Sheila and Jane nodded approvingly. I felt like I'd made the right choice by sharing that unique example.

As the interview wrapped up, Jane said, "Thank you, Jaideep. We appreciate your honesty and the insights you've shared with us today. We'll be in touch soon."

Gabriele added, "We know you're leaving for India soon, so we'll try to expedite the decision process. Safe travels, and we'll keep you posted."

"Thank you both. I appreciate the opportunity and look forward to hearing from you." I said, relieved it was over.

I closed my laptop and leaned back in my chair, feeling a mix of exhaustion and cautious optimism. The interview had gone better than I'd feared. Now, all I could do was wait.

I decided to distract myself from mulling over the interview by getting back to packing. Within an hour, I had everything sorted. Then, as I often did when I felt uncertain, I started talking to the images of God on my desk, asking for guidance and hoping for a miracle. Deep down, I knew that God only helps those who help themselves, and I felt I hadn't exactly given my best in that interview. So, I couldn't really blame anyone but myself if things didn't go my way.

Around 4 p.m., Gabriele rang. This time, instead of the usual anxiety, a wave of positivity rushed through me. I answered the call, trying to keep my voice steady.

Without much preamble, she asked, "Jaideep, what are your salary expectations, and when can you start?"

I quickly replied, "AU$60K per annum, and I can start in three weeks from now, the day after I return from India."

"Great." she said. "I'll get back to you shortly."

As I hung up, a sense of confidence settled in. I knew I'd asked for a reasonable salary—nothing too high, but not below the standard either.

Just 20 minutes later, my phone rang again. Gabriele.

"Congratulations, Jaideep!" she said. "You've been selected for the job."

I felt an overwhelming sense of relief and excitement. The weight of my financial worries began to lift as I understood that all my hard work and perseverance had finally paid off.

I immediately called my family to share the good news, and they were overjoyed. My parents expressed their pride, and Amar congratulated me. This felt like a turning point, not just in my career, but in my life.

With the job secured, I started to think about my upcoming trip to India in a new light. What was initially a journey filled with uncertainty was now a well-deserved break before starting my new role. I looked forward to spending time with my family and reconnecting with my roots, while knowing a promising career awaited me upon my return.

After I finished my call with my family, I quit my casual work at Traffic Australia for good, feeling grateful for the opportunity it provided during a tough time. Then I got a contract from Gabriele, confirming my start date and any final details about the job.

During my last evening in Australia before the trip, I took some time to reflect on my journey—the struggles, the doubts and the unexpected opportunities that came my way. I recognised how much I had grown, not just professionally, but personally.

On the day of my departure, I felt a mixture of excitement and nostalgia as I boarded the plane to India. The flight felt different this time; I was no longer the student or the intern struggling to make ends meet. I was now someone with a career, a future and a sense of accomplishment.

My time in India became a period of rejuvenation. Surrounded by family, I enjoyed the warmth and comfort of home, which I'd missed so much. I spent my days catching up with old friends, enjoying home-cooked meals and simply relaxing.

However, even during this break, I kept my eye on the future. I started researching the role I'd be stepping into, reading up on industry trends and preparing myself mentally for the challenges ahead. The vacation gave me the perfect balance of rest and preparation, setting the stage for a strong start in my new job.

I also contacted my childhood friend Suyash, who lives in Sydney.

"Hey, Suyash! I've got some great news—I landed a full-time job!"

"Congrats, man!" he replied, genuinely happy for me.

"Thanks! I'm actually thinking of moving from my old place. Do you know any good spots?"

"Well, funny you ask." Suyash said. "I'm living at Sydney Student Living in Burwood, and I'm looking for a roommate. It's a really happening place, with around 200 people living here. We all hang out and have a great time together."

"That sounds perfect." I said. "I could really use some company after living such a lonely life lately."

"Awesome! It'll be great to have you here." he said, and I felt a wave of relief and excitement.

As the three weeks in India came to an end, I felt ready and excited to return to Australia. When I boarded the plane back, I did so with a renewed sense of purpose. I was eager to start this new chapter, knowing that everything I had worked for had led me to this point in my life.

As I reached Sydney Airport, my phone buzzed with a message from Suyash: "Hey, I'm near the airport. We can head to our new place together."

I immediately called him back. "Hey, Suyash! I just got off the plane."

"Perfect timing." he said. "I'm waiting near the arrivals terminal. I'll see you in a bit."

After passing through immigration and picking up my baggage, I spotted Suyash. We greeted each other, and without wasting any time, we boarded the train and headed straight to Sydney Student Living, ready to settle into my new home.

As the train pulled into Burwood station, I felt a mix of anticipation and curiosity. After a short walk, Suyash and I arrived at Sydney Student Living in Concord. "This is it." Suyash said with a smile as we stood in front of the entrance. "Welcome to your new home."

The building loomed large, buzzing with energy. The place was alive with students, some chatting in groups, others hurrying to their rooms or the common areas. I could already sense the vibrant atmosphere that Suyash had mentioned.

As we walked through the front door, the first thing that caught my eye was the reception area, manned by a friendly-looking bald guy. Suyash introduced him as Sava.

"Welcome! You must be his new roommate." Sava said with a warm smile. "Let me show you around."

"Thanks, Sava. Looking forward to it."

We dropped off my luggage in my room, conveniently just next to reception. After making sure everything was in place, Sava led us to the barbecue and pool areas. The vibe was lively, with people chatting, laughing and playing table tennis. Clearly, this place had a strong sense of community.

"Looks like a great spot to unwind." I said, taking in the atmosphere.

Sava nodded. "It is. We often have barbecue nights here. You'll get to know everyone pretty quickly."

Next, we moved on to the common areas, where a group of students was focusing on a game of FIFA on Xbox. Suyash chuckled, "This is where we all hang out when we're not studying—or even when we should be studying."

I smiled. "I might join you guys for a game sometime."

After that, Sava showed me the communal kitchen. It was well-equipped and spacious, with a few students already preparing meals. "After you cook, you must clean the utensils then and there. If you don't, the fine is $50." Sava said.

"The fine hasn't changed with inflation in the past four years." I said.

"What?"

"When I first came to Melbourne four years ago, I used to live in accommodation shared by 24 people. Even there the fine for not doing the dishes was 50 bucks." I said.

"Now that you point it out, I realised we haven't changed it either in the past few years." Sava said and walked towards the door at the other end of the kitchen.

Next, we went to inspect the laundry, then the study area, which had a quiet, focused ambiance—perfect for getting work done. "And here's the gym." Sava said as we headed down to the basement.

"Not bad." I commented. "This is the only place that makes me feel that I don't belong here."

Finally, we climbed a flight of stairs to reach the rooftop terrace. The view was breathtaking; the Sydney skyline stretched out in the distance, its lights just beginning to twinkle as the sun set.

"This view never gets old." Suyash said, leaning on the railing.

I nodded, taking it all in. "I can see why. It's incredible."

The tour ended with a dinner where I met more of the residents—my new friends. We shared stories and laughter, and by the end of the night, I felt like I was already part of the community.

As I lay in bed later that night, I felt both excitement and contentment. Tomorrow, I'd start my new job, but tonight, I was happy to have found a place that already felt like home.

I woke up, excited and ready to start my new job. I knew this job could shape my life for better or worse. I got ready in record time, my mind buzzing with thoughts of the day ahead. I left the house early, aiming to reach the office by 8:30 a.m., well before my 8:45 reporting time.

When I arrived, I found the office still closed. I sat down by the door, trying to stay calm, but the wait only fuelled my anticipation. A few minutes later, I heard footsteps approaching, and then I saw Laura. She smiled as she unlocked the door with her access card.

"Morning, Jaideep." she said warmly as she opened the door.

"Morning, Laura! Thanks for letting me in." I replied, stepping inside.

"No problem at all. You're early—good start!"

We exchanged a few pleasantries as I walked in, feeling more at ease now that I was inside the office. At last, the day was beginning.

The view from the office was spectacular. As I looked through the large windows, I could see the sparkling waters of Sydney Harbour stretching out before me. The gentle waves lapped against the timber piers, and boats of all sizes dotted the horizon, their sails catching the morning light. The iconic Sydney skyline stood tall in the distance, with the Harbour Bridge gracefully arching over the water, a constant reminder of the city's vibrant energy.

The sunlight danced on the water's surface, creating a mesmerising pattern of light and shadow, constantly shifting. The view made me stop and take a deep breath, appreciating the beauty around me. The air was crisp and carried a hint of salt from the sea, adding to the invigorating atmosphere. This was more than just an office—it was a place where the city's pulse could be felt, where every glance out the window reminded me that I was now part of something much bigger.

As I was admiring the view, Sheila walked in with a cheerful "Hi, Jaideep!" startling me. "Sorry for scaring you." she laughed.

"I'll introduce you to everyone shortly. But first, let's go over your responsibilities and how things work around here."

We headed to the meeting room where I'd had my interview. Once seated, she asked, "How was your commute to the office?"

I told her, "It's about a 45-minute door-to-door trip. Just one train from Burwood station to Town Hall, and then a walk through the city and across Pyrmont Bridge. The atmosphere on the bridge was incredible—people enjoying their day, and the cool breeze blowing across really helped ease my nerves and gave me the confidence I needed. I want to excel at this job, just to keep enjoying this view every day."

She smiled, pleased. "Not everyone appreciates that, but I'm glad you do."

She went on to explain the company's operations. "As a shipping company, we play a crucial role in the country's economy. We need to be fast and diligent, ensuring our ships run at full capacity. For that, you need to be smart and proactive. Proactivity will come with experience, so it's important that you learn as much as possible, as quickly as possible. Don't hesitate to ask for more work. Everyone here has been at this for a long time, and they'll appreciate any help you can offer. The energy you bring to the office will be the key to your success. Results may not always be in our control, but the effort we put in is. I expect nothing less than 100 percent from you."

I assured her, "I'll give my 120 percent. If I ever fall short of your expectations, please feel free to tell me. I'm adaptive and can make quick changes to benefit the organisation."

After we discussed my daily tasks, Sheila mentioned, "There's been a recent development regarding your position. Initially, it was a one-year contract role, but now it's been made a full-time position. When I checked with HR about this change, Gab mentioned that your visa is only valid for another year and a half, and you're working on your PR. To ease some of the pressure on you, here's what we suggest: start strong in your work, and off work, focus on your PR. Once you obtain it, let us know, and we'll work on extending the role."

This news lifted a huge weight off my shoulders. Seeing the relief on my face, Sheila wrapped up our session and then introduced me to everyone before taking me to my cubicle to get settled in.

With renewed energy and a sharp mind, I began my training, shadowing each team member as they carried out their tasks and taking detailed notes on how to complete the various assignments we received via email. They also shared valuable insights on communication, especially since we dealt directly with customers. Hours flew by as I moved from one desk to another, immersing myself in the workflow. At lunchtime, the team dispersed for a bite and I went out to search for the nearest migration agents. Fortunately, I found one just 100 metres away. I called and inquired about his availability for assistance with my PR application. He asked me to visit his office at 5:30 that evening. After a quick lunch at a nearby café, I returned to the office, eager to be back before the team resumed our training session.

At 5 p.m., people started to leave the office. I stayed behind to chat with any colleagues still there, until everyone had departed. Then I left to go to the immigration lawyer's office.

METHOD TO MY MADNESS

The immigration agent's office was in a modest space tucked away just 100 metres from my work. The receptionist greeted me warmly and guided me to a consultation room. A professional-looking gentleman entered moments later.

"Good evening." he said, extending his hand. "I'm Kevin. You must be Jaideep."

"Yes, that's me." I replied, shaking his hand. "Thank you for seeing me on such short notice."

"Not a problem at all. Please, have a seat." he gestured towards a comfortable chair. "So, how can I assist you today?"

"I'm interested in applying for permanent residency under the Skilled Occupation List." I began. "I'm currently employed as a sales-support representative at ANL, and I wanted to understand the process and see if I'm eligible."

He nodded thoughtfully. "Let's start by assessing your eligibility. May I ask about your age, educational background, and work experience?"

"Certainly." I said. "I'm 27 years old. I have a master's in engineering management, a bachelor's degree in electrical engineering and more than two years' work experience in supply chain management."

"Excellent! Electrical engineering is in demand right now as the government wants more electrical engineers. There are more slots available under electrical engineers." he replied, making notes.

"That's very good. When I originally applied for engineering, I wanted to do mechanical, but I got into electrical engineering."

"There's hardly any production in Australia, so demand for mechanical engineers is very low. Being an electrical engineer is good for your application. And have you taken an English proficiency test, like IELTS (international English language testing system) or PTE (Pearson test of English)?"

"Yes, I took the IELTS three years back and scored an overall band of seven."

"That's a good score." he said, "but have you something more recent? Those scores are only valid for two years. You'll have to do these tests again. I would suggest the PTE because it is much easier to score an eight band in PTE than in IELTS."

"Noted, Kevin." I said. "I'll prepare for PTE then."

"Have you accredited your overseas bachelor's degree with Engineers Australia, yet?"

"No, not yet."

"Do you know what it is?"

"Not entirely sure; can you please clarify?"

"All overseas education must be accredited by an Australia body to verify its authenticity. In other parts of the world, many people can actually *buy* a qualification."

"Not a problem."

"And you can prove that by getting your degree accredited by Engineers Australia. You have to write three career episodes about three different projects you have undertaken under electrical engineering or as an electrical engineer. There's more information on career episodes available on the Engineers Australia website."

"I can do that."

"Based on your background, it looks like you can meet the basic requirements in the coming months. We'll need to calculate your points to be sure. The minimum threshold is 60 points if you want to apply for PR as an electrical engineer."

He pulled out a points-assessment sheet and began tally-ing. "Age: 30 points. Local education for two years: five points. Skilled employment: since you have worked less than three years, you will not get any points for that."

"That means I only have 35 points."

"If you can score a seven band in PTE then you will get 10 more points and when you get your bachelor's degree accredited, that will give you additional 15 points. That would bring you to a total of 60 points."

I felt a surge of relief. "So, right now, I just meet the minimum requirement?"

"Yes, but if you can score an eight band in PTE, that'll give you 20 points, instead of 10 when you score the seven band. That will bring your score to 70 points, and this is a very competitive score." he said. "The higher your points, the better your chances of receiving an invitation to apply."

"That's great to hear." I said, smiling. "What are the next steps?"

"First, you'll need a positive degree assessment from Engineers Australia."

I nodded. "How long does the skills assessment process take?"

"Typically, it takes about eight to 12 weeks." he explained. "Simultaneously, you will need to prove your English profi-ciency." Then he continued as I was making notes, "Once we have a positive skills assessment and PTE score, we can submit an Expression of Interest (EOI)."

"And after submitting the EOI?"

"Then we wait for an invitation to apply for the visa." he said. "Invitations are issued monthly, and your points score will place you favourably in the selection process."

"Understood." I said. "Are there any other requirements I should be aware of?"

"You'll need to meet health and character requirements." he added. "This involves a medical examination and police clearance certificates from any country you've lived in for more than 12 months in the past ten years."

"That shouldn't be a problem." I replied. "Could you also outline your fees and services?"

"Of course." he said, handing me a brochure. "Our fees cover the entire application process, including the skills assessment, EOI submission and visa application. We offer personalised guidance to ensure all your documents meet the required standards."

I glanced over the brochure. "Thank you, PR application fees is $3600, degree assessment is $1200, the PTE is $300 per test and your consulting fee is $11,000."

"Yes. Do you have any more questions?"

"What are my chances of success?"

"While I can't guarantee an outcome, your profile is strong, and with careful preparation, you have a very good chance."

"That's reassuring." I smiled. "Just one last question, while I work on my skill assessment and English test, you'll just submit my application, right?"

"Correct."

"Why can't I do this myself then?"

"If you think you can do it yourself, then proceed with that. If you have any questions, you can always contact us. Remember, this is your first consultation, so it will only cost you $50. If you wish to make any more appointments, charges will be $250 per 45-minute session."

"That sounds good to me. Thanks for all this information."

We shook hands, and I left his office with a renewed optimism about my future in Australia.

After leaving Kevin's office, I felt a mix of determination and exhaustion. The train ride home gave me some time to think. With my next steps clearly laid out—book the PTE test, the skills assessment, and plenty of other tasks—I began organising my thoughts, making a mental checklist of everything I needed to do. The weeks ahead were going to be intense, especially juggling all this with my new job. But I knew I had to stay focused.

When I finally reached my new place, I decided to unwind a little and headed to the barbecue area. That's where I met Ajeet, another resident, sitting by the benches when I walked over. After introducing myself, we started chatting.

"So, you're new here?" Ajeet asked.

"Yeah, just moved in yesterday." I replied, "and today was my first day at my new job."

Before Ajeet could respond, a white guy walked into the barbecue area and headed straight for the ping-pong table, paddle in hand. Ajeet chuckled and leaned in closer to me.

"That's Ryan." he said in a low voice, with a mischievous grin. "He's from Crystal Brook in South Australia. The town population there is less than a building population in Mumbai. Apparently, two weeks ago, he ran out of body wash, and since then, he's been using shampoo for everything. Dude's been showering with it ever since."

Ajeet had that kind of humour that made even the simplest things sound hilarious. I burst out laughing, picturing the scenario. Ryan noticed us and wandered over, clearly curious about what was so funny.

"What's up, guys?" Ryan asked. "How's your day been?"

I smiled, still amused. "It was good. First day at a new job, actually. Spent the day training with the team and then headed to a migration agent's office afterward."

"Migration agent, huh? Sounds serious." Ryan replied, nodding as he leaned against the table. "You applying for PR or something?"

"Yeah." I said. "I'm trying to apply under the Skilled Occupation List. Just had my first consultation today."

"Man, that process can be a pain." Ryan said. "My friend went through it a few months back. It's a lot of paperwork, but you seem on top of it." He sounded more positive about me than I was.

"I'm doing my best." I chuckled. "Kevin, the agent, gave me a long to-do list. Need to work on my skills assessment and take the PTE exam again, since my old IELTS score expired."

"How'd the first day at work go?" Ajeet asked.

"Pretty good. Still learning the ropes. It's a lot to take in, but I'll get the hang of it. I'm just trying to balance everything, you know? Work, the PR process ... it's going to be tough."

"Tell me about it." Ryan chimed in. "I remember my roommate doing the same thing—working full time while trying to get all the documents in order for the PR. You gotta make good use of your weekends. That's the only time you'll have to really focus."

"Exactly!" I agreed. "I work nine to five, so weekends are my only time for this. I just booked the PTE exam, but the next available slot isn't for another two months. Meanwhile, I'll be working on my skills assessment with Engineers Australia. It's all about finding the balance."

"Sounds like you've got a solid plan, though." Ajeet said.

"Yeah, I've mapped it out. It's just a lot to juggle." I replied, feeling the weight of it all but reassured by their understanding nods.

Ryan glanced at the ping-pong table. "Well, if you need a break from all that juggling, hit me up for a game of ping-pong. Trust me, it helps." he said, flashing a grin.

I laughed. "I might just take you up on that."

As the conversation wound down and the night grew quieter, I felt more grounded. Meeting Ajeet and Ryan reminded me that I wasn't alone in this journey. Everyone had their own challenges; we were all just figuring things out together.

The next morning, I woke up feeling both motivated and stressed. It was my second day at the new job, and I knew the learning curve wasn't going to slow down soon. The team was helpful, but every task seemed like a mountain to climb. Still, I had no choice but to push through—this job was my key to stability in Australia, at least for now.

On my way to work, my mind was constantly jumping between the tasks I had to complete for the PR application and my responsibilities at ANL. At the office, the day passed in a blur of training sessions, emails and meetings. I barely had time to catch my breath. During lunch, I pulled out my notebook to jot down a quick to-do list for the PR process—call Engineers Australia, begin drafting my career episodes and research prep for the PTE exam.

By the time 5 p.m. rolled around, I felt drained, but also proud. I was managing to keep both worlds—work and PR—moving forward. On the train ride home, I reviewed Kevin's checklist once again, adding notes about the next steps for my skills assessment.

When I arrived at my place, Ajeet was in the barbecue area again, chatting with Ryan. They waved me over, and soon I found myself laughing with them about random things—Ryan's quirky habit of using shampoo for everything was still a source of endless amusement. I briefly allowed myself to relax, putting the day's stress behind me.

"So, how's the PR grind going?" Ryan asked as he tossed a ping-pong ball back and forth with Ajeet.

"Slow and steady." I replied, stretching my arms. "I've booked the PTE test for two months from now, and I'm starting on the skills assessment. But between that and learning my new job, it feels like I'm working two full-time gigs."

"You are." Ajeet said with a sympathetic smile. "It's rough, but you've got your plan, right? Just stick to it, man."

"Yeah, I know." I nodded. "It's just the waiting part that's killing me. Two months for the PTE test, and then eight to 12 weeks for the skills assessment. Everything moves so slowly."

"That's the Australian way." Ryan said with a grin. "But hey, at least once it's done, it's done. You just have to survive the waiting game."

"I'll survive." I said, more to myself than to them. "I have to!"

The first weekend in Sydney, I woke up early, determined to kick-start my PTE preparation, but life had other plans. My laundry basket was overflowing, so I had to deal with that first. I went down to the reception and luckily, Sava was on duty.

"Morning, Sava. Can I get some change for the washing machine?" I asked.

He smiled and handed me the coins. "Here you go, mate. How's your first week been?"

"Pretty good." I replied. "Just settling in and, you know, getting used to the new job and everything."

He nodded, and I went back to my room. But when I got there, I saw Suyash was still fast asleep. Not wanting to disturb him, I decided to hold off on the laundry, and went to the barbecue area instead, figuring I could at least enjoy some fresh air and clear my mind before diving into study.

As I sat there, a group of people began gathering around. I introduced myself, and soon I was chatting with Jamie from Iran, Macky from Israel, Barry from the Netherlands, and Sammy and Anup from India. Everyone had their own unique story, and the vibe was friendly and relaxed. We exchanged laughs and talked about our experiences so far in Australia.

Mid-conversation, Sava walked into the barbecue area, looking directly at me with a grin on his face. "Hey, didn't you get change from me for the laundry about an hour ago?" he asked, raising an eyebrow.

I chuckled nervously. "Yeah, but Suyash is still sleeping, and I didn't want to disturb him."

At that, everyone burst out laughing. "What? You're waiting for him to wake up?" they all exclaimed.

Sava shook his head, amused. "Right, that's it." he said. "Follow me, guys. We'll sort this out."

Intrigued, everyone stood up, following Sava as he led the way back to my room. When we arrived, Sava pulled out a master key, and with a quiet but swift move, he opened the door. We all crept in, taking positions around Suyash's bed, holding back our laughter. With a signal from Sava, everyone grabbed one limb—each person carefully taking an arm or leg—and at the count of three, we all lifted him up.

Suyash shot upright, his eyes still closed, his face a mixture of shock and confusion as he wobbled to his feet. Before he could even process what was happening, they grabbed his mattress and propped it up against the wall, leaving him with nowhere to fall back asleep.

He stood there, completely bewildered, while the rest of us doubled over with laughter. As we left the room, I caught a glimpse of his face—still half-asleep, his eyes barely open, trying to piece together what had just happened. His expression was priceless, like someone who had just been dragged out of a dream and thrown straight into chaos.

Back at the barbecue area, the laughter continued. "You can thank Sava for that wake-up call." I said to Suyash, grinning.

"Hey, I was just trying to help you get that laundry done!" Sava replied, still chuckling.

With that, I finally went to the laundry, threw my clothes in the washing machine and returned to my group of new friends. We spent the next hour chatting about the randomness of shared living spaces, the quirks of roommates and the odd but funny situations we found ourselves in.

It was the perfect way to unwind from the intense week I'd had—meeting new people, sharing laughs and briefly escaping the pressure of work and the PR process.

But even as the laughter faded and the morning rolled into afternoon, the reality of my situation didn't fade. With laundry done and the barbecue winding down, I headed back to my room. Suyash was finally up, rubbing his eyes, still recovering from the shock.

"Man, what just happened?" he asked groggily, still in disbelief.

"Just your friendly neighbourhood wake-up squad." I replied with a grin. "You can thank Sava for that one."

He shook his head, smiling. "I'll get him back for that, just wait."

I knew this weekend was exactly what I needed. The upcoming weeks would be busy and filled with stress, but making new friends and finding humour in small things helped to keep me grounded. And with my PTE test two months away and my skills assessment looming, I knew I had to make the most of every light-hearted moment before diving back into the grind.

The weekend flowed by quickly, and Sunday night arrived with that familiar mix of dread and anticipation for the week ahead. I sat on my bed, scrolling through my phone, thinking about the tasks I had lined up for Monday. Work was picking up pace, and with every passing day, I was getting more involved in my new role. Balancing that with the PR process meant that my schedule was now packed, and I knew I had to stay organised if I wanted to pull this off.

By Monday morning, I was back into the routine—wake up early, eat a quick breakfast, and head to the office. The team was supportive, and I was learning quickly, but the amount of information I had to absorb was overwhelming. My days became a blur of emails, client calls, shadowing team members and jotting down every piece of advice they gave me. Each task felt like a small victory, but exhaustion was starting to creep in as the pressure started to build.

My evenings were spent researching Engineers Australia, reading up on how to get my bachelor's degree accredited and preparing for the PTE exam. I had to figure out how to complete a crucial part of the skills assessment: writing my career episodes. These were detailed reports on projects I'd worked on during my electrical engineering studies. Each episode needed to be clear, precise and demonstrate my skills as an engineer.

It was tough. Some nights, I stayed up late, trying to recall the specifics of projects I hadn't thought about in years. Other times,

I felt the strain of trying to focus after a long day at work. But I kept reminding myself why I was doing this—why I'd made the decision to apply for PR in the first place.

As the days passed, I kept running into my new group of friends—Ajeet, Ryan, Jamie, Macky, Barry, Sammy, and Anup—whether it was in the barbecue area or just around the building. They became a regular part of my week, and the laughs and conversations we shared were the perfect escape from the daily grind.

One evening, after work, I found myself back at the barbecue area, a cold drink in hand, watching Jamie practising his table tennis serve. While doing that, he mentioned that he was from Iran. Ajeet wandered over, dropping his bag on a nearby chair.

"Another day, huh?" Ajeet said, leaning back and stretching. "How's the PR stuff going?"

I sighed. "Honestly, it's overwhelming. Work is non-stop, and then there's all this PR paperwork. I feel like I'm constantly juggling things, and I'm worried something's going to slip."

Jamie, overhearing, spun around and pointed his paddle at me. "Mate, you've got time. Just take it one step at a time. That's what I did when I applied for citizenship. It feels like a lot, but you'll get through it."

"Yeah, easier said than done." I muttered, taking a sip of my drink.

Ajeet nodded. "I get that. But you've already made a plan, right? You booked the PTE test, you've started the skills assessment. You've got this."

"Yeah, but there's so much I don't know yet." I said. "I'm still trying to figure out how to write these career episodes for Engineers Australia. They're supposed to show how I meet the criteria as an electrical engineer, but it's hard to put all that technical stuff into words."

"Sounds like a pain." Macky said, joining us. "But hey, maybe this weekend you can take a break, play some table tennis, clear your head. Sometimes a break is all you need."

I laughed. "Maybe you're right. I could use a break."

We spent the rest of the evening sharing stories, but in the back of my mind, the to-do list was still there—looming, waiting for my attention.

As the weekend approached, I planned my next steps carefully. Saturday morning would be dedicated to drafting the first of my career episodes. I decided to focus on the project I had done during my final year of university, where I'd worked on designing an illumination system with LEDs. I knew this challenging project would highlight my skills as an electrical engineer.

The weekend came, and I was at my desk early Saturday morning, laptop open, ready to write. The laundry was already done (no more sleeping roommates to wake up), and with a coffee by my side, I dived into the details of my project. The words didn't flow easily at first, but after a few hours, I had a solid draft of my first career episode.

Later that day, I bumped into Sammy and Ajeet at the barbecue area again. "How's the writing going?" Ajeet asked.

"Slow, but I've got one episode down. Two more to go."

"That's progress, man." Sammy said, giving me a thumbs-up. "Keep at it."

I nodded. The encouragement helped more than they knew. This process was a marathon, not a sprint, and while the road ahead seemed long, I felt a little more confident knowing I had friends around me.

As I headed back to my room that evening, I couldn't help but feel a sense of accomplishment. A lot of work lay ahead— both at my job and for my PR—but for the first time in a while, I felt like I was on track. Little by little, I was making progress, and that was all that mattered.

The following week also flew by in a blur of work, meetings and late nights. My routine settled into a steady rhythm: 9 to 5 at work, evenings spent tackling the never-ending to-do list for my PR application, and whatever time I could spare for socialising with my new friends. The balance was hard to maintain, but I had to keep pushing forward.

By Friday, I was completely drained. Work had picked up, and I'd been assigned more responsibilities as I grew more comfortable with my role. I could feel the pressure building, but I kept reminding myself that the hard work would pay off. My weekends were my lifeline—the only time I could fully focus on preparing for the PTE exam and progressing with my skills assessment.

Saturday morning, I woke up early again, determined to tackle my second career episode. This time, I planned to write about a group project I'd worked on during my study for the bachelor's in electrical engineering—creating a smart grid system to optimise energy usage in a small community—a perfect project to showcase my engineering skills.

But just as I was about to open my laptop, I heard a knock at the door. Ajeet, with a wide grin on his face.

"Mate, we're heading to the beach today. You in?" he asked.

I hesitated. The beach sounded like the perfect escape from the stress, but I also had a lot to do. "I don't know, man. I've got this career episode to finish for my skills assessment."

Ajeet gave me a knowing look. "You've been working non-stop. You deserve a break. Plus, the weather's perfect. A few hours won't hurt."

I thought about it. A part of me wanted to stay in and keep working, but the idea of some fresh air and sunshine was tempting. Finally, I gave in.

"All right, you convinced me." I said, grabbing my bag. "Let's go."

We met the others—Ryan, Macky, and Barry—at the barbecue area before leaving for Bondi Beach. The sun was shining, the sky was clear, and as soon as we arrived, I felt a wave of relaxation wash over me. I'd made the right decision.

The beach was packed, but we found a spot to spread our towels. Ryan and Macky immediately headed for the water, while Ajeet and I stayed back, chatting as we watched the waves.

"You've got a lot on your plate, man." Ajeet said, glancing at me. "But don't burn yourself out. I've seen people crash and burn trying to do everything at once."

"I know." I sighed. "It's just hard. I feel like there's always something more to do. Work, the PR application … it never ends."

Ajeet nodded. "I get it. But you've got to pace yourself. You'll get there. And hey, at least you're not doing it alone. You've got us."

I smiled, feeling grateful for the friendships I'd made. It was true—I wasn't doing this alone. Having people around who understood the challenges of navigating life in a new country made a world of difference.

After a couple of hours at the beach, we grabbed some fish and chips from a nearby stand and sat down on the grass to eat. The conversation drifted from work to travel, and eventually, to life in Australia. Barry shared stories about his adventures around the country, and Ryan entertained us with tales of his small-town life in Crystal Brook. I laughed more than I had in weeks.

When we finally headed back, I felt recharged. The break had been exactly what I needed. And though I still had work to do, I knew I could approach it with a clearer head and a better mindset.

That evening, I sat down at my laptop and began working on my second career episode. This time, the words flowed more easily. The day at the beach had given me some much-needed perspective, and I found myself able to focus without feeling overwhelmed.

By the end of the weekend, I had two solid career episodes completed, and I felt more confident about my progress. There would be testing times ahead, but finally, I felt I was managing everything better.

The next couple of weeks followed a similar pattern. I finished my third and final career episode, reviewed it carefully, and prepared to submit it to Engineers Australia for the skills assessment.

The PTE test date was approaching as well. I started dedicating more time to preparation, focusing on improving my speaking and writing skills. I felt the pressure building again, but knew I was on track. The light at the end of the tunnel was getting brighter.

One evening, after another long day at work, I ran into Ryan in the hallway. He noticed the stress on my face and gave me a sympathetic smile.

"Hang in there, mate." he said. "You're almost through the worst of it."

"I hope so." I replied, rubbing my tired eyes. "I just want this to be over."

"It will be." he assured me. "And when it is, we're celebrating. Drinks on me."

I chuckled. "Deal."

As I headed back to my room, I felt a renewed sense of determination. The journey wasn't easy, but, step by step, I was getting closer to my goal. And with the support of my friends, I knew I could get through whatever came next.

The next morning, I woke up with a sense of urgency. It was the weekend, and I had exactly one month left before the PTE exam. With my skills assessment submitted, my focus shifted fully to preparing for the exam. I'd downloaded practice materials, bookmarked helpful videos and joined a couple of online forums where people shared tips for scoring well on the PTE. But no matter how many times I told myself I was on track, the nerves kept creeping in.

I picked up my laptop and headed down to the barbecue area, my usual spot for studying. The fresh air and the sound of distant conversations helped me focus better than being cooped up inside. As I set up my study materials, Sammy wandered over with a coffee in hand.

"Morning!" Sammy said, taking a seat across from me. "What are you up to?"

"Just preparing for the PTE exam." I replied, glancing at my notes. "Got one month left."

"Man, you're really going for it." he said, nodding. "But you're smart. You'll ace it."

"I hope so." I said, though I appreciated the encouragement. "There's just so much pressure, you know? It feels like everything hinges on this test. If I don't score well, I won't get enough points for my PR."

Sammy leaned back and took a sip of his coffee. "I've heard a lot of people say that about the PTE. But from what I've seen, it's all about strategy. You just need to know the test format inside out."

"That's what I keep reading online, too." I said. "I'm focusing more on the speaking and writing sections because they're where I can score the most points. But the listening part—man, it's tricky."

"Yeah, I've heard that, too." Sammy agreed. "But look, just pace yourself. You've got time."

We chatted a bit longer before Sammy had to leave for work, and I returned to my practice tests. The hours flew by as I went through question after question, honing my skills and building confidence. But by the time the sun set, I'd spent almost the entire day on PTE prep. My head was spinning with strategies, tips and sample answers. I needed a break.

That night, Ajeet, Ryan and some of the other guys planned to eat dinner in the city, and they'd invited me along. I hesitated, thinking I should spend more time studying. But then I remembered what Ajeet had said the week before—balance is key. I had put in the work, and I deserved a night off.

We met at Nilgiri's, a popular Indian restaurant in the city, the smell of spices and grilled meats filling the air as we walked in. The conversation was light-hearted as we ordered a variety of dishes to share. Sava, true to form, kept the table entertained with stories of his life in New Zealand and Canberra, while Macky gave us a glimpse into his earlier life in Israel.

As the night wore on, I found myself relaxing more and more. The weight of the PTE and PR process faded into the background for a few hours. I knew how important it was to give myself time to recharge, to enjoy the journey, even when the destination felt far away.

On the way back home, Anup nudged me. "You seemed more relaxed tonight. Good to see."

"Yeah." I admitted. "I needed that. I've been stressing over this exam for weeks, but tonight was a good reminder to take it easy sometimes."

"Good." Anup replied.

As my PTE exam date approached, I could feel the tension rising again, but I stayed disciplined. I spent my evenings revising speaking prompts, perfecting my essay structure and taking practice listening tests.

Finally, the day of the PTE exam arrived.

I woke up early, my heart racing. Everything I'd worked for over the past two months came down to this moment. After getting ready and reviewing my notes one last time, I went to the test centre. The streets were quiet as I walked, and I used the time to calm my nerves, reminding myself that I'd prepared as best as I could.

The exam itself was intense. The oral section flew by in a blur, and the writing prompts were tougher than I expected, but I powered through. When the listening section came, I did my best to stay focused, picking up on every detail I could. By the time I reached the reading section, I was mentally drained, but I pushed through, knowing the finish line was in sight.

When I finally walked out of there, I felt a strange mix of relief and uncertainty. I'd done everything I could, but now it was out of my hands. The results would be available in a few days, and until then, all I could do was wait.

I texted Ajeet and Ryan to let them know the test was done, and almost immediately, they replied with plans to meet up for dinner to celebrate. It wasn't a guaranteed win yet, but just making it through the exam felt like a victory in itself.

Over dinner that night, the guys cheered me on, sharing their own stories of stressful moments and how they got through them. Their support meant the world to me, and for the first time in weeks, I allowed myself to fully relax.

The waiting period for the PTE results felt like an eternity. But when the email finally came, I hesitated before opening it. The next few minutes would determine my next steps.

I took a deep breath and clicked on the message. A perfect score—an eight band in every section. I had done it!

My heart raced with excitement. This was it. I was now at 55 points.

The next six weeks felt like a blur of "work hard, party harder." Between juggling long hours at ANL and letting off steam with friends on the weekends, there wasn't much time or energy for anything else. The waiting, though, was always at the back of my mind—waiting for the results from Engineers Australia, the last piece of the puzzle before I could apply for PR.

Every so often, I'd log into my immi account just to make sure everything was still in order. I wanted to be ready as soon as I got my skills assessment result. When it came time to start my application, I planned to finish it in one go, with no delays.

By the sixth week after receiving my PTE results, I was checking my email out of habit when I saw the message I'd been waiting for, from Engineers Australia.

My degree had been accredited!

A rush of relief and excitement hit me. This was it—the final step had been completed. With the positive skills assessment in hand, I now had the 15 additional points I needed to reach 70. I quickly calculated everything again: age, local education, PTE results, and now the skills assessment—all adding up perfectly.

As soon as I saw the confirmation from Engineers Australia, I didn't waste a second. I opened my immi account, heart pounding with anticipation.

I meticulously filled out the required forms, double-checked every detail and uploaded all the relevant documents: my accredited degree, PTE results, work experience letters, and identification. Everything was in place. Finally, with a deep breath, I submitted my EOI.

The satisfaction that followed was unlike anything I'd felt before. All the hard work, sleepless nights and doubts had led to this point. I'd done everything I could, and for the first time in a long while, I felt at peace. Now, all I had to do was wait. The ball was in Immigration's court.

With the EOI submitted, my only real worry now was paying off my education loan. I was paying it off on time every month but it was taking 40 percent of my salary. It was frustrating to struggle with money but I reminded myself that patience was the key. I knew it could take a few months to receive an invitation to apply for PR, but I had crossed the biggest hurdle. Now, it was just a matter of time.

As I closed my laptop, I leaned back and let the sense of accomplishment sink in. The journey wasn't over yet, but for the first time in a long time, I felt like I could finally breathe.

———◦◦◇◦◦———

Within the next six months, I received the email I had been waiting for—my invitation to apply for PR. I promptly paid the PR fees and was granted a bridging visa. The process was moving forward, and though there were still a few more steps, the hardest part was behind me.

One Saturday morning, as I was still anxiously waiting for news on my PR application, things felt different. Sammy barged into the room, a burst of energy as usual.

"Hey, Jaideep! Suyash! Let's go for a photoshoot at the Opera House!" he announced with his usual grin.

I blinked, surprised. "Opera House?" I repeated, the words stirring something in me.

"Yeah, man! Let's go! You've been in Sydney this long, and you haven't seen it yet? It's a crime!" Sammy laughed, already packing his camera bag.

It hit me then—I'd completely forgotten about the Opera House. I'd always dreamt of visiting it, but somehow this had slipped through the cracks of my daily grind.

Suyash rolled over in his bed, groaning. "Photo shoot? It's Saturday, man. Sleep day."

But I was already up, the idea of seeing my dream place pulling me out of my fatigue. I'd seen the Harbour Bridge plenty of times from my office window, its iconic steel arch in the distance, but the Opera House—never in person.

"Let's do it!" I said, suddenly feeling excited.

A couple of hours later, the three of us were at Burwood station, heading to Circular Quay. The train ride felt different that morning, as if it was taking me not just to a landmark but to something symbolic—an experience I'd longed for, something that reminded me why I chose this path to Australia in the first place.

As the train moved through the city, my mind wandered back over my journey so far—the endless paperwork, the exams, the long hours at work, and now, waiting for that one email that could change everything.

But today, at least for a few hours, I could let it all go. Today was about seeing the Opera House for the first time.

The train rumbled along, and when we got off at Circular Quay, I was immediately struck by the energy of the place. The station buzzed with activity—tourists with cameras slung over their shoulders, locals heading to ferries and street performers filling the air with music. But none of that mattered. I walked towards the exit. There it was, in the distance, rising above the harbour like a vision.

The Sydney Opera House.

I'd seen it countless times in pictures and videos, but standing there, looking at its gleaming white sails reflecting the morning sunlight, it felt unreal. The design was unlike anything I'd ever seen—bold, sweeping curves that seemed to defy gravity, set against the backdrop of the sparkling blue water of the harbour. It was more than just a building; it was a symbol of the city, of Australia itself, and here I was, seeing it for the first time.

"Wow." I muttered under my breath.

Sammy clapped a hand on my back. "Told you, man! You can't live in Sydney and not experience this in person!"

The closer we got, the more surreal it felt. The sails, so crisp and sharp from a distance, revealed their intricate and delicate tiled texture up close. The harbour breeze carried the sound of water lapping against the shore and I could hear the faint hum of the ferries coming and going.

Suyash, now fully awake and smiling, simply nodded. "It's impressive. But we're here for the photoshoot, remember?"

We walked closer, the Opera House growing larger, more real with every step. Sammy, already snapping photos, was in his element. I watched as people moved around the forecourt, tourists posing for pictures, some sitting on the steps just soaking it all in.

As we neared the Opera House, a strange sense of calm washed over me. For the first time in weeks, the constant hum of anxiety about my PR process seemed to fade. I let myself get lost in the beauty of the moment.

I couldn't help but feel a sense of awe. It wasn't just the size or the beauty of the Opera House that struck me, but the fact that I was here—thousands of miles from home, standing in front of one of the world's most recognisable landmarks.

"Let's get a shot of all of us." Sammy said, pulling out his camera.

We lined up, the Harbour Bridge in the background and Sammy set the camera on a timer. The three of us stood there, smiling, as the camera clicked away.

After a while, we sat down by the water, looking out at the boats moving across the harbour. It was so peaceful.

"Isn't this what it's all about?" I said, more to myself than to anyone else. "Moments like this."

Sammy glanced over, raising an eyebrow. "You're getting all deep now, man."

I laughed. "I just needed a reminder. I've been so caught up in work and the PR stuff that I forgot to enjoy where I am."

"You'll get it." Suyash said, looking out at the Opera House. "The PR, I mean. You've worked too hard not to."

"I hope so." I said, letting out a breath. "But today, I'm just going to appreciate this. The PR will come when it comes."

Sammy lifted his camera again, capturing a few more shots.

I smiled, feeling lighter than I had in weeks. We sat there for a long time, just soaking in the beauty of the harbour, the Opera House behind us like a symbol of everything I had worked for— freedom, opportunity and a future in a place I'd come to love.

For the first time in a long time, I was just … here. Living it.

Then, four months later, on a regular Friday afternoon at work, something extraordinary happened. I was appreciating the view from my desk when a notification popped up on my phone from Immigration. My hands trembled as I opened the message.

"Your Permanent Residency has been granted."

I couldn't believe it. After all the hard work, the waiting, and the uncertainty, it had finally happened. The first thing I did was call my dad and mum. Their joy and relief were palpable through the phone. Then, I called Amar, my younger brother, and shared the news. He was over the moon, almost as excited as I was.

As soon as I wrapped up work, I headed straight to SSL. Sammy and Ajeet were the first ones I met by the pool area. Without saying much, I pulled out my phone and showed them the visa grant letter. Their faces lit up, and we quickly rounded up the rest of the crew. Once everyone had gathered, we shared the news, and only one thing was left to do: party.

That night was wild! We danced at the club like there was no tomorrow, celebrating, soaking in the achievement I'd worked so hard for. It was a night of pure joy, laughter and unforgettable memories.

The next morning, I woke up with the worst hangover, but the happiness from the night before still lingered. After freshening up and having something to eat, I sat alone in my room, opened the email and re-read the visa grant letter.

Alone with my thoughts, it felt surreal. I'd turned a dream into reality, and I knew that the journey ahead was just beginning.

As I read it, emotions welled up inside me. My heart felt like it was bursting, and I felt a single tear slide down my cheek.

My lips quivered as I whispered to myself, "I wanted it. I didn't know I could do it, but I worked for it. And I *did* it!"

EPILOGUE

"Hello, I'm Jaideep. My wife Rutuja and I are here to meet Georgio. We have an appointment with him to discuss buying an apartment in Parramatta." I said to the receptionist as we stepped into the builder's office.

The receptionist smiled and gestured to her right. "Go ahead. He's expecting you."

We followed her direction and entered Georgio's office. After a warm handshake and brief pleasantries, we got straight to business, discussing the apartment details and financials. As the conversation wrapped up, Georgio leaned back in his chair and asked, "So, where are you guys originally from?"

"Mumbai, India." I replied. "And what about you? Your name sounds Italian, but you've got quite an Aussie accent."

Georgio chuckled. "My grandfather made a wise choice when he moved to Brisbane back in the late 1950s. Honestly, I'm grateful he did. My life wouldn't be what it is today if he hadn't."

"But Italy is a good country too, isn't it? It has its own charm and plenty of opportunities." I said, intrigued.

"It is, and it does." he said, "but the gap between the rich and the poor is immense. I'm just thankful I grew up here. It's given me a lot more stability and opportunities."

I nodded in agreement. After thanking Georgio for his time, we visited the display apartment and then began our walk back home.

"I didn't come to Australia in search of a better life." I said to Rutuja as we strolled down the tree-lined street.

"So why are you telling me this?" she asked.

"What if our children—or even our grandchildren—think we moved to run away from something?"

She paused, then shrugged. "We can't control what others think about us, Jaideep."

"No, we can't." I admitted. "But I can try to make sure my story—our story—will stand the test of time and last for generations."

Her lips curled into a teasing smile. "And how do you plan on doing that?"

"I'll write a book."

ABOUT THE AUTHOR

Jaideep Padalwar is a first-time author whose journey to writing has been anything but conventional. With an academic foundation in electrical engineering and a career in the corporate world, Jaideep has always been a seeker of meaning beyond the confines of spreadsheets, presentations and emails.

Born in India, he grew up navigating a world of expectations and aspirations, and this experience deeply influenced his debut book, *Engineering the Australian Dream*. He started writing it to document a series of personal struggles, but along the way it evolved into a series of accomplishments, showing his relentless pursuit of a dream to stay in Australia.

His brother's unwavering support also played a significant role in shaping this book.

Jaideep embraced the challenge of writing, finding joy in transforming life's complexities into stories of achieving success. He wants to encourage others to see life as a series of opportunities waiting to be grasped.

When he's not writing or working, Jaideep can be found exploring new ideas, spending time with loved ones, or enjoying the occasional escape into sports or outdoor adventures.

Engineering the Australian Dream is a testament to the power of perseverance and self-belief—a reminder that it's never too early to create something meaningful.

www.ingramcontent.com/pod-product-compliance
Lightning Source LLC
Chambersburg PA
CBHW022118080426

42734CB00006B/172